Not an Englishman

NOT AN ENGLISHMAN

*Conversations
with Lord Goodman*

DAVID SELBOURNE

SINCLAIR-STEVENSON

First published in Great Britain in 1993
by Sinclair-Stevenson
an imprint of Reed Consumer Books Ltd
Michelin House, 81 Fulham Road, London SW3 6RB
and Auckland, Melbourne, Singapore and Toronto

Copyright © 1993 by David Selbourne

The right of David Selbourne to be identified
as author of this work has been asserted by
him in accordance with the Copyright,
Design and Patent Act 1988

A CIP catalogue record for this book
is available at the British Library
ISBN 1 85619 365 9

Typeset by CentraCet, Cambridge
Printed and bound in Great Britain
by Clays Ltd, St Ives PLC

After a certain age a new friend
is a wonder, like Sarah's child.

W. M. Thackeray

Contents

Introduction

Between June and November 1992, Lord Goodman and I met – at his house in Oxford or his flat in London – on twenty-three occasions, and conducted the conversations of which this book is the result. These conversations themselves grew from earlier, less formal discussions which we had been having intermittently during the previous five years, until the point was reached when I felt, such was the quality of what he was saying to me *en passant*, that I should proceed more systematically than hitherto and take a note of his remarks for the record.

The majority of the topics treated here were thrust upon him for the most part without notice; nor did G., as I call him throughout this book, receive any forewarning of the questions I intended to ask him. ('If you had told me in advance what you wanted to talk about,' G. said on one occasion, 'I should have spent the intervening time preparing and worrying about my replies.') This made more remarkable the fluency and coherence of his answers, the readiness of his analogies and examples, the precision of his *mots justes* and the thought-out quality of his opinions.

In the span of five months G. could not avoid all contradiction, but he was normally able to deny it with considerable deftness, 'distinguishing' between one proposition and its seeming contrary with the acumen of the best of lawyers. 'I have never known a man escape with such intellectual skill from a contradiction in his argument, real or apparent,' I said to him, at which he beamed. 'You have the skill of a Houdini,' I added, at which I thought him less pleased. But he was at his intellectual best when his judgments were challenged, and drawn to his sharpest thoughts when under pressure.

The order in which the topics are presented here is the order in which we discussed them; my notes were taken in a swift enough long-hand; not all the material of our conversations has been used in this book; there has been no retrospective rethinking or rewriting either on G.'s part or mine; and such contradictions as there may be have been left to stand. These are discussions, not finished essays.

Nevertheless, I was constantly struck by the spontaneous shapeliness of G.'s reactions to taxing questions. What, I once unreasonably asked him, is 'pure love'? His answer, delivered without a moment's hesitation and as if without effort, was not a sentence but a paragraph of lucid prose. 'Parental love, maternal love in particular,' he said, 'is as pure a love as you can find. It is instanced in children's confidence in their parents and tested by the fact that at a time of danger parents will rescue them before they think of their own safeties. Such love is rarely motivated by self-interest, except in the case of a desire to produce a good child. But, particularly in Jewish mothers, parental love is too often associated with boasting about the virtues of the children.'

This is not to say that a conversation with G. proceeds without difficulty. Some of his positions are well-guarded, and upon them he may not easily be engaged. In such cases I was driven to circle about, alternately leading with a right or a left in an effort to draw him from his corner. G. showed himself to be swift-minded and fertile in expression, but as agile (and elusive) in side-stepping an issue when he chose, as bold in confronting it when he chose. He was scrupulous in answering, or attempting to answer, questions in the terms in which they were formulated. But if the terms were maladroit, the question (especially at first asking) might not be answered at all.

G. was also adept in parrying questions with levity or broad humour; in hedging himself around with irony and wryness, including at his own expense; sometimes in taking refuge behind a barricade of orotundity, a veil of witticism, or a smokescreen of mere words. But more often, and rarely with hesitation – I have noted the occasions – he addressed himself directly and with trenchancy to what I asked, following the questions wherever they might lead, and not retreating from the outcome.

The resonances in some of G.'s answers were often profound: it was the moral philosopher in him (as well as the 'good mind' of an 'astute lawyer' according to more conventional, and not always wholly friendly, judgment of him) who was increasingly disclosed as our conversations moved from topic to topic. There are close parallels – sometimes to the word – between G.'s preferred principles of behaviour and those laid down by the Jewish sages. 'Take care,' declares *Deuteronomy*, 15.9, for example, 'lest there be a wicked thought in your heart . . . and your eye be malevolent towards your brother, the needy one.' In reproach of greedy acquisitiveness, dishonesty or unscrupulous ambition, as in praise of hospitality and friendship, there are ancient accents in G.'s discourse. The virtues of Cicero's 'good and worthy man', as recommended to his son Marcus in the *Offices*, include sagacity in giving advice, liberality, a judicious eloquence, knowledge of the law, dislike of ambition and a readiness to help others.

When G. spoke in disparagement of himself – or, at least, in tongue-in-cheek disclaimer of his own merits – there were other echoes from the depths of our moral culture. 'I can consider myself better than some others,' Kant declares in one of his Lectures on Ethics, 'but it is not very much only to be better than the worst, and there is really not much moral pride in that.' The terms of G.'s attack – in chapter four – upon the medical profession recall the similar sentiments of the (part-Jewish) Montaigne, in his *Essays*: there were no people, Montaigne thought, 'so confident as those who entertain us with fables, such as your alchemists, judicial astrologers, fortune-tellers and physicians.' Of this judgment, William Carew Hazlitt wrote that 'it must be borne in mind that . . . in the time of Montaigne . . . the general body of so-called physicians were mere empirics and charlatans.' In G.'s view, so it seemed, many of them still are.

In what follows, G. also tells his wartime tale – familiar to his friends – of his exchange with a sergeant who had taken him aside and asked him in confidence whether a third person was a Jew: 'he is not, but I am,' G. had replied. There is a classic tale to match this also. When Count Anton von Auersberg visited the poet Heine in Paris in November 1837, he complained to the latter, of all people, that most of his [von Auersberg's] entourage were Jews. 'I am always embarrassed when I want to ask one of them whether another is a Jew,' the Count earnestly told Heine. 'For it is more than likely that the man I ask will himself turn out to be Jewish.'

Indeed, it is the Jewishness of G. about which least bones are made in his conversation; in its way, an object-lesson for meeker Jewish spirits, of whom I am one. A Ciceronian ethic there may be, and certain judgments which other men in other times have uttered. But it is G. the Jew, and a Jew of most particular qualities, who addressed me in our conversations. The 'clever' Jew? The 'astute' Jew? The 'learned' Jew? The 'successful' Jew? The 'liberal-minded, humane' Jew? 'The East End Jew made good'? All of these (or perhaps none of them), but something else besides: the 'Court Jew' or *Hof-Jude* of (yet another) classical tradition, with the greatest of whose number G. must be counted.

In the roles of privy councillors, diplomatic and legal advisers, court bankers and factors, and (even) as physicians, distinguished Jews in the historic past – from the courts of the Renaissance to those of the Kings of Prussia, to go no further – have wielded large and merited influence in high places. Like G., Adolphe Crémieux, the great Franco-Jewish lawyer of the mid-nineteenth century, was a modern incarnation of the genus. One of the spokesmen of the 1848 revolution – and described by De Tocqueville as 'ugly and eloquent' – Crémieux was a *bon vivant*, a lover of art and music, horses and the theatre, who defended the poor and the persecuted.

As Professor S.S. Prawer sets out in *Heine's Jewish Comedy*, the poet considered that the qualities necessary to be a Court Jew included a quick and penetrating intelligence, versatility, inventiveness and an ultimately pessimistic outlook on life. G. is not, or claims not to be, a pessimist; but in other respects Heine would, I believe, have recognized G.'s character and public role well enough. But G. must also be, in his persona of latter-day Grand Vizier, one of the last of the Mohicans as adviser to the princes and princelings of the British realm: there are more likely in future – even in a newly anti-semitic age

– to be eminent Jews of due capacity and standing than princes for them to advise.

G. would disown such encomia of him. More than once during our conversations he expressed anxiety about the 'vanity' of having his passing observations preserved in book form. Nevertheless, for all his disclaimers, I would be tempted to describe him as among the greatest of living Englishmen – if he had not denied, several times over, that he was an Englishman at all.

On Being a Jew

I started talking about Jewishness as a burden – even, in Heine's sense, as a malady for which a cure needed to be found. (In fact, Heine thought the malady to be incurable, except perhaps by time.) G. said, 'It puzzles me that anyone should regard being Jewish as a problem.' Yes, but some do, I commented, and it is surely rare for Jews to deny it. 'It is really anxiety about the reaction of others,' he said; it was not a feeling in the individual Jew that Jewishness itself was a burden. Moreover, it was an issue 'contaminated', as he put it, 'by the Christian approach to the Jews.' But you must be among the very few Jews who don't feel, or don't appear to feel, the consequent burden of this approach, I said to him. 'No doubt there is a certain arrogance in my attitude,' he answered phlegmatically. 'But being a Jew is a fact of life, about which you need not worry.

'I feel this partly because I have enjoyed the good fortune of living in a country as free as could be.' Perhaps, but are you saying that there is no anti-semitism here? 'I myself have not encountered any prejudice, although this possibly arises from a skill in evading it. In my experience, such prejudice is more frequently found in Jews against other Jews.' But even if you feel none of the unease which most other Jews feel about themselves, you must at least acknowledge that *they* feel it. 'If some are ashamed of being Jewish, in Britain it is out of a particular sense of inferiority. They do not regard themselves as being inferior to Turks, Eskimos or Hottentots but only as inferior to English Christians.' You mean that they feel at a disadvantage in face of a certain kind of English manner? 'Yes, because they admire it.'

You say you have never encountered anti-semitic prejudice, but I have, I said. What would your reply be to someone who, not knowing you to be a Jew, referred to a third person as a 'Jew boy', as has happened to me? 'I would have said to him,' G. replied without a moment's hesitation, ' "If you had known I was a Jew, I cannot believe you would have made a remark in such bad taste." '

This, I said, is Olympian in a fashion to which most Jews cannot aspire. My father, for instance, was aroused to indignation and aggression by anti-semitism; or, at least, by the belief that an individual was actuated by it. He would near clench his fists with the desire – at least in the telling – to knock such an individual's block off. 'I'm nearly 80. I'm not in the business of knocking people's blocks off,' said G., laughing. 'I'd probably end up having my own block knocked off.'

I was still unable to accept that his life had been entirely free of the experience of anti-semitic sentiment. He then recalled how, when he was in the Army, a sergeant had asked him in confidence whether a third person was a Jew. The sergeant was astonished when G. pointed out that the *other* man was not a Jew, but that he was. 'I would have thought,' G. added, 'that I am a noticeably recognisable Jew.' His entire calm on the subject, however, was outside my experience; belligerence and anxiety are surely commoner, and also more natural, Jewish reflexes. 'If you are a member of any minority,' he continued, 'the important thing is not to go looking for trouble, because if you do you'll soon find it.'

Yes, but this attitude could also seem to other Jews like the avoidance of a duty to stand up to prejudice and open hostility. 'What else can you do?' he asked me quizzically. But your response suggests that Jews make a fuss about nothing, and that anti-semitism is a figment of their imaginations. 'There is no anti-semitism among the aristocracy. It is the upper middle-classes who are the most fiercely anti-semitic,' he said, contradicting the tenor of his earlier remarks, 'because they resent Jewish competition. The Jews do not compete with the dukes, the countesses and the earls. They compete with the doctors and the lawyers. And what makes it worse is that they compete successfully.' Nevertheless, such anti-semitism seemingly does not provoke you in the way that it provokes some others – they are capable of feeling it viscerally. 'I've been very fortunate in my career,' he said briefly.

Are you implying that it is your special virtues that have enabled you to prosper without arousing such feelings in others? 'One is mistaken to compliment oneself on that.' But you are suggesting something like it, or at least you convey the impression of having found the secret of avoiding the pitfalls which some Jews at least encounter in their professional careers. 'It might be,' he said, weighing the matter, 'that I have a certain mental agility in sensing early, and sidestepping, disagreeable circumstances which might have unfortunate consequences.' Don't you have any sympathy with those who feel embattled, however subconsciously, over anti-semitism as a result of being Jewish? 'They search it out.' He here referred to a Jewish businessman of his acquaintance who 'yearns for anti-semitism, because it justifies him': a fierce judgment.

But your philosophy might seem, to some, to be simply that of 'avoiding trouble'. How was such an attitude to your Jewishness formed in you? Is it something you came to gradually? 'My mother was much more emphatic and assertive in her Jewishness than my father. She would have fallen upon anyone who made an anti-semitic remark in her presence.' But you wouldn't do such a thing. 'I never look for quarrels. I do not think there is anything to be gained from controversy. You won't convert the anti-semite, and the sin of the Holy Ghost is to lose your temper.' You mean you never lose your temper? 'Very rarely. One occasion I can recall is when a relative made a disparaging remark about my father.' I can understand that, but how can you go so far as to say that there is nothing to be gained from controversy? Isn't it the stuff of debate, of democratic argument and so on? 'What I mean,' he said, 'is that anything which leads to your voice being dominated by emotion should be avoided.'

This is either the impossible advice of a saint, or the secret of your great reputation for sagacity, I said to him. 'Perhaps it is,' he said.

I asked G. if being Jewish was more important to him than anything else. 'That is like asking whether the wallpaper on the wall is more important than anything else in the room. It is there. I do not know that I am acutely conscious of it. But if I was cross-examined I would have to admit that it has an influence. That influence is very difficult to define. My life has not led me along specifically Jewish paths. That is not to say I do not recognise its importance. But I do not think I view anything specifically as a Jew.' But hasn't your role in public life as councillor, as peacemaker, as adviser to the powerful been very similar to that of Jews in the historical past? 'I cannot comment on that. That is for others to say. If I have come to occupy such a role, it is something which I cannot seek to analyse, nor can I say how far it has been affected by my being a Jew.'

What are you then? I asked. How would you describe yourself? [At this point, his housekeeper brought in coffee and he waited until she had gone out before answering.] 'I am not an Englishman, but a Jew born in England. I owe a debt to England, I have had every conceivable reward in England that I could have hoped for, but I do not regard myself as an Englishman.' I am surprised to hear, I said, that you do not consider yourself an Englishman; you must therefore think that there is some difference between you as a Jew and an Englishman who is not a Jew. 'I detect a difference between my way of thinking and an Englishman's way of thinking.'

What difference? 'First of all, it is a reflex. I do not, however, associate any problem with an exclusively Jewish answer. There is not a Jewish answer to every problem.' But if you as a Jew think differently from an Englishman by 'reflex', there must be such a thing as a 'Jewish answer'. 'A Jew would provide an individual answer,' said G.. Why? 'Because he is not an Englishman.' A fine circular argument, said I. 'I know,' G. said, laughing.

What is this Jewish 'reflex' to which you have referred? 'The principal reflex is when you scent anti-semitism. However, it is necessary that that reflex should not operate without proper justification. It is very possible for some Jews to go in quest of anti-semitism merely in justification for themselves in some piece of behaviour. That is wrong and dangerous.' But the 'difference' which you detect between yourself and an Englishman is surely elusive? What is it to be a Jew, in your judgment? 'It is the clear-cut and unambiguous recognition that you are a Jew. The form of this recognition is different with every Jew. But it has not played an obtrusive part in my life.' This Jewishness of yours, I said, has a rather indefinite quality about it, all in all. 'It is not a quality, but a background,' he said; (like his wallpaper). 'It is less important in my life than other things. I am not uneasy about being a Jew. To a great number of Jews, the question of their Jewishness obtrudes because they are unhappy about it.'

Are you yourself proud, then, of belonging to this 'particular' people, as the Bible calls them? 'I do not pride myself on it, because I am not responsible for it,' he answered in his most wry fashion. Can you say that you are 'less Jewish' than your father and mother? 'I am less Jewish than my father, though he was not particularly pious. But he was a great Hebrew scholar, which I am not. He spent most evenings reading Hebrew books. My mother – who had dogs, not a very Jewish characteristic – was a teacher, gave private Hebrew lessons, and spoke Yiddish, but not at home. My father preferred Hebrew. He had an anxiety that we should learn it. Mr Schneiderman, a Hebrew teacher, came twice a week to teach my brother and I, using the Hebrew bible as a basic literature.' So you can read Hebrew? 'I can read Hebrew and understand synagogue prayers better than most. But inevitably I am less Jewish than my parents were, even though they were not devout. My life led me away from being Jewish. My six years in the Army, for instance, led me away; I joined up before war broke out.'

G.'s father, who was an East End shipping broker and whose own father came to England from Lithuania, was greatly respected and had a reputation in the Jewish community as a peacemaker, a role which G. said he had 'to some extent inherited'. 'My father had great difficulty in persuading us to go to synagogue. He led an austere way of life, drank rarely, and smoked like a chimney. I do not think my father and mother – whose essential characteristic was tolerance – ever went out to a restaurant. There was a beautiful simplicity about my father's life. He abhorred ostentation.'

Yet the Jews are sometimes seen by non-Jews as 'pushy', 'vulgar' and so on, I said. Have you yourself tried to avoid being this archetypal Jew? I ventured. 'Never,' he said with great vehemence. 'I would be ashamed consciously to avoid it.' Do you feel recoil from, say, a Jewish criminal like Maxwell? Do you feel anxiety as a Jew about being contaminated by association? 'I have some sense of recoil from such people as individuals', G. replied. 'But my first reaction is not that "bad Jews" contaminate all of us. It may be my unshakeable sense of superiority that I do not feel it,' he added, chuckling. 'In any case there is such a variety of conceptions of the Jews that anybody can say anything about them.'

But if you are 'less Jewish' than your parents, doesn't this imply that you have gone some way towards 'assimilation'? At this G. bridled. 'I deeply resent those who have consciously left their faith,' he said by way of answer. 'It is cowardice, snobbishness and a ridiculous reaction to one's birthright.' Perhaps, but not all Jews, especially those less privileged and more uncertain than you, see it that way. 'I have one friend who is in particular deeply embarrassed by it. But the motive is spurious. Such people have an unjustifiable sense of being ashamed.' What is the source of this 'embarrassment', as you see it? 'They sense a general hostility to Jews and do not want to be included in that sense,' G. answered.

Yet you are a liberal Jew by practice, and have yourself rejected, or discarded, a large part of what other more orthodox Jews would regard as essential features of Jewishness. 'I cannot say that I don't ride on buses on Saturday because I don't ride on buses on any day of the week,' he said, beaming. So what kind of Jewishness would you say you had chosen for yourself? 'An acceptable form of Jewishness which one can offer to anyone to whom the rigours of Judaism are beyond their capacity to endure,' he replied sardonically.

But these 'rigours' are what many, perhaps most, Jews, at least in theory, consider to be the right sort of Judaism? 'The old rigours,' he said, 'are the right sort of Judaism. But I prefer an alternative which leaves a sense of balance.' Then you have made a compromise between being a Jew and being an Englishman, haven't you? 'No,' G. replied, 'between being a Jew and being sensible.' So what is this Jewishness? 'Decent and not too onerous', he cheerfully replied. Nevertheless, to some Jews you are barely a Jew at all. 'The orthodox regard me as an apostate. They cannot find words strong enough to condemn me,' he said merrily. Don't you mind? 'It leaves me indifferent,' he said.

Would you agree that you've made your own Jewishness for yourself? 'Certainly,' G. answered. 'Everybody does. But if there was a determined onslaught on the Jews, I would be the first to enlist in their defence.' Do you believe in God, I asked, or the Messianic return? 'I do not believe in the return of the Messiah. If He was coming, He would have returned a long time ago. A place at the Seder [Passover] table has been left for Him for centuries, and even [laughingly] a portion of chicken.' What about God? 'I believe that some force must have brought the world into existence.' Explanation for the 'perfection of a leaf', said G., required an 'originating' design, a force which 'must have been there to get it all started', a force which he also called 'someone'.

As for resurrection, heaven and hell, an after-life of punishment and reward, G. said: 'I do not disbelieve in them, but I never think of them actively. I hope I do not commit villainous acts, but I would not be deterred by hell-fire if I did.' I called his religion a 'selective business'. 'So is Catholicism,' he replied briefly, 'so is Islam.' Are there any aspects, especially moral aspects, of Christian belief to which you are attracted? I asked. 'Christianity, in my view, is a great deal of nonsense.' ('But I wouldn't want that published,' he added.) But surely you don't dismiss its entire ethic? 'I am totally unimpressed by Christianity. I do not believe in its miracles or in Christ. The Sermon on the Mount is a marvellous prescription for behaviour, but it does not mean that you can elevate Christ to be the Son of God.'

Is it not, however, a generous creed in certain ways in which Judaism is not? 'It may be a generous creed, but I do not believe in miracles, or that Christ walked on the water. I have never met an eye-witness of the event, so I remain sceptical about it. Above all, I am bitterly opposed to Christians who try to proselytise among the Jews.' [On an earlier occasion, however, G. had said something different about this: that Jews should not get exercised over proselytisation, since those Jews who were tempted to conversion other Jews should be glad not to have among their numbers.]

It sounds, I said, as if you think that Jews are 'better' than Christians. Are they? 'The simple answer is "yes",' said G. 'I apply a moral test. They are more generous. The ones I deal with I can single out as being more honest and more trustworthy.' But if you have chosen to deal with them, then they are a select sample. 'The Jews,' he insisted, 'have the edge.' But isn't there a greater scoundrelliness among Jews in money matters? He shook his head. 'It is true,' he continued, 'that the Jews have a tremendous interest in money, because it is the index of security. Some of my very rich [Jewish] friends who won't give anything to anybody feel that history makes it unwise for them to do so. They never know when they might need their resources.'

Are you saying that you haven't encountered miserliness or avarice among Jews? 'I could give a hundred examples of it. But its root cause is insecurity. It lies in the belief among many Jews that wherever they are settled they cannot consider it as permanent.' Some non-Jews might think that special pleading, said I. 'I don't care what non-Jews – or Jews for that matter – think of my opinions. Of course, I would hate to think that my views aroused hostility in decent people. One of Harold Wilson's great weaknesses was his inveterate habit of looking over his shoulder before he did anything for fear of how others might judge him. I regard that with contempt.' Yes, but your own sagacity, I rejoined, must be composed in part of shrewdness, and even – not using the term pejoratively – of 'calculation'. Don't you yourself look before you leap?

'I am not athletic enough to leap,' G. jestingly replied. 'But on the whole I give rather less thought to the consequences of my actions than most people. If I think a situation requires redress I am more prone to act than most people. That argues a high degree of self-satisfaction on my part,' he added. 'But I do not wake up in the night counting my imperfections.' Do you wake up in the night counting your perfections? I asked. G. laughed. 'I do not do that either. That would be a waste of sleep.'

Do your principles derive from something you know to

be a Jewish morality? I asked, getting back to the subject of our conversation. 'The consciousness of being a Jew has a relatively small influence upon me,' he repeated. 'I don't think that being a Jew is of paramount importance to me.' But aren't your Jewish friends the closest friends you have? 'Inevitably the *oldest* friends I have are those who go back 75 years, two in particular. Both of them are Jewish. But some of the friends who go back to my teens are Christian.' Do you feel more comfortable with the former than the latter? 'Every Jew feels more comfortable with other Jews when Jewish matters are under discussion,' he replied, side-stepping the question. What about in other respects? 'If I wanted assistance,' he answered, 'I would seek out a Jew.' By 'assistance' do you mean moral support? You can't mean financial assistance, surely? 'Moral assistance I do not need, but I would not seek out a rabbi if I did,' he said, laughing.

But can you imagine ever needing financial assistance? 'I have never enjoyed total financial security,' G. replied, 'although my standards may be more demanding than others'. I have ended up in a reasonably satisfactory situation. I have my flat in London, this house [in Oxford] and an income sufficient for my needs. But I never had any real interest in money, and I never sought material success. The outcome is probably more satisfactory than I deserve,' he added, wryness returning. 'My brother left me what he owned, and I turned it into a charitable trust which enables me to give away £20,000 per annum to good causes.' Nevertheless, I said, you are still anxious about the possibility of indigence? 'I do not know that I have ever had material success sufficient to render apprehensions about poverty unnecessary,' he replied elaborately. Is this the Jewish insecurity you spoke of? 'It is universal, particularly among the bourgeoisie or the middle class, who are not supported, or imagine they are not supported, by adequate resources.'

Has your anxiety about money arisen from the fact that the friends you have had made it necessary for you to live in a certain style? 'I never thought it necessary to live in a certain style. The person who thought that I should was Jenny Lee. She was then living in Ashley Gardens, and I had found a small flat in the same building. She said to me one day, "You ought to have a better flat now that you are chairman of the Arts Council." I was also never "anxious about money"; I never had any feeling that I would not earn an adequate living. I was always conscious that I had a living. Some very kind people also left me pictures.'

Were your parents 'poor'? 'By the standards of the rich, yes,' he answered, 'but they looked after us well.' I recalled how at my father's death – his own parents were East End Jews – a collection of silk handkerchiefs and perfumed soap had been found hidden away in his study; the things, I said, which had once represented the unattainable to him. 'I have been able to do things in an expensive way,' was G.'s comment. 'I travel First Class – or Club Class – and I stay in the best hotels because I enjoy it.' He called such indulgences luxuries. 'But I must say that I have never had any respect for riches as such. I also do not pity a man because he is poor.'

It surprises me that you should say that, I commented, when you have a reputation for coming to the aid of the underdog. 'Not if no efforts on his behalf would make him an overdog,' said G. What do you mean? 'I have no conscious sympathy for anyone whose way of life is enjoined by his own behaviour. I do not rush in to sympathise with the afflicted. I like to see what the causes are.' Some of what you are saying surprises me, I repeated.

'I would feel uneasy in turning away someone who came to me in some need. ['A man would have to be of very evil behaviour before I cast him out,' he said later.] But I could not present myself as the Haroun-el-Raschid of the day. I greatly approve of charity,' he added, 'but that, of course, is a Jewish instinct.'

Yet not all Jews are charitable, as you have said yourself. 'Many are, many are not.' But, according to you, more Jews than Christians, proportionately? 'I would not deny that. The very denial says something, says too much,' G. declared, meaning that to deny it was to accuse Jews of miserliness, which G. in turn denies.

As I had listened to him today, his role as the reincarnation of the Jewish Grand Vizier, or 'Court Jew', of historic times became plainer than ever. 'I have not played as prominent a part as others may claim,' G. insisted. 'But all in all it has been a benign part.' Are you conscious of the sage Jews in positions of eminence who have gone before you? He took this question to refer to Britain, and brought up the name of Disraeli. He described him as a man who had 'left the fold' but who 'retained sympathy for the Jews all his life'. But since he chose the way of baptism and abandoned his faith, said I, presumably he does not have your approval. 'He abandoned his faith,' replied G., 'but he had no choice;' it had been, he said, 'done by his father'.

But for you, was it not a 'contemptible' deed? 'My contempt is only for those who act in this way for social reasons,' G. said. Nevertheless, I take it that Disraeli's life is no model. 'He is a man who became a Christian,' G. answered, 'became a political animal, and became the leader of the feudal aristocracy. I never had any aspiration to lead the feudal aristocracy. I do not think they would have followed me even if I had.' But although you

13

disapprove in principle of 'social' baptism, not everybody has been so fortunate as you as a Jew, nor had your self-assurance. Heine became baptised in the hope of obtaining a German professorship. 'I do not think anyone would be so foolish now as to abandon his faith for a professorship,' said G. with a chuckle.

'If your father was a Jew, and his father too, and his father's father, you have no right to abandon this heritage,' G. then declared. But surely you yourself have abandoned it to some extent? After all, there is no sense of taboo in you about a ham sandwich. 'I am not intimidated by Jewish dietary laws,' claimed G.. 'I have no sense of wrong about such matters, and am not apprehensive of the hereafter wagging its finger at me about what I have eaten. If Judaism is not eating bacon, or eel, or lobster, or crayfish, or crab, or not travelling on a Saturday, it is not worth a ha'penny.'

It was, he argued, rabbinical Judaism which he had rejected, not 'ethical Judaism'. Nevertheless, I said, the nature of your Jewish belief still remains hard to identify. 'It is very rare to find a Jew who knows what he believes in,' responded G. with good humour. Perhaps it is best to call the Jews a race, and leave it at that? 'I would give some support to that. But it is more a strong sense of preserving the Jewish image and the Jewish tradition.' What about the ham sandwich? 'That has nothing to do with the Jewish tradition.' The Chief Rabbi wouldn't agree. 'I am not impressed by fanaticism,' said G..

So what is the irreducible minimum of Jewishness? 'It lies in acknowledging the fact that you are a Jew, that Jews differ from other people, and that you have a duty to the Jewish community and to other Jews.' That is precisely what some non-Jews would think of as the 'Jewish conspiracy'. He shrugged. 'If non-Jews want to entertain such outrageous views about the Jews, so be it.' Yet you say they 'differ from other people', a sentiment which many non-Jews resent. 'They do not differ in every way. They are more charitable, as I have said, and they respect education far more than they respect rank. My father would not have got up from his chair to welcome a duke, but he would have got up to welcome a scholar.'

But now the Jewish community had 'lost 150,000 or more' since G.'s younger days, 'although very few through conversion.' Do you bemoan the rate of intermarriage? I asked. 'It is taking a risk,' he answered. 'My mother' – whom he now called a 'good orthodox Jewish mother', when he had earlier described her as 'not devout' – 'said that she would much rather I married a Christian than that I did not marry at all. At the time I had a Christian girlfriend. "If what's stopping you is that you think I'd disapprove," she told me, "that is not so." Subsequently, she urged me two or three times in particular directions [that is, towards two or three girls], but I had no appetite for them.' Was she disappointed, as a 'good Jewish mother', that you did not marry? 'She was disappointed by my lack of heirs,' G. replied.

Friendship, Love and Honour

We began to speak of friendship, a topic G. had earlier said he wished to discuss, and I recalled how he had once said to me that the English had little taste for it.

'You have to approach the subject with caution in England,' he declared, 'because it makes the British uneasy. They regard such terms as "dear friend" as an affectation and react to them with embarrassment.' Such friendships as exist, he said, were 'cultivated, for example, by the idiotic public school system', in which young people were 'immured' in 'strangely reactionary and primitive institutions'. In such institutions a 'sense of companionship' was 'inculcated among the victims', but under conditions of duress and from the need for mutual support. The kind of caring such conditions fostered could be 'sincere', but it was 'to some extent involuntary'; it was friendship as a forced rapport, even if the individuals 'sincerely wished to be friends.'

True friendship was different. 'I can't define it,' said G., 'but the expression in Britain of the emotions of friendship would cause embarrassment to a great number of people. I am not trying to elevate the significance of friendship to a level it cannot sustain, but the Roland-and-Oliver type of friendship does not exist in England.'

Can you really assert such a thing? 'When the British embark on a dangerous and difficult operation, like Scott of the Antarctic, then there is team-spirit. The man who left the tent, Titus Oates, was moved by a genuine desire to save his colleagues.' But, to G., this stoicism – a reflection of the spirit of the public school and the temperament it produces – was distinct from the emotion of the real friend. I asked him whether he was saying that the emotional capacity for a deeper kind of friendship than this public school kind did not exist among the English? 'You wouldn't find it,' he answered. 'You might find a couple devoted to each other out of homosexual temptation. You can have relationships based on admiration or jealousy; the basis might be 101 different things. But the emotional element of true friendship is at variance with the British temperament. It is an embarrassment.' Do you reproach the English for this? 'You can reproach them. Emotions are always a difficult matter for the English, I am afraid. Emotion at Armistice Day, for example, is obviously largely synthetic, but good enough for the occasion.'

Are you saying there is something *wrong* with the English which is peculiar to them? 'I would resist that suggestion. To adapt Shylock, if you prick them they bleed. But you *have* to prick them for them to feel anything, and pricking them with a pin is generally not enough. In many ways, the English are very cold fish. This does not, however, negate the valuable qualities they possess, foremost that of tolerance, particularly for the Jews.' But how would you explain their temperament? Is it historical, geographical or what? I asked him. 'It is not historical; it has always been there. It might be the climate or the food,' he answered, laughing. 'But to whatever the absence of emotion in the British character is due, it is certainly there. The hated French above all assert it. They like to point to that coldness, or aloofness, of which the British themselves, strangely enough, are proud, as if it were some quality they had gained by practice, or as if they had earned it by their achievements. It is tied up with patriotism. Only certain demonstrations of feeling are justified. The English, for instance, stand to attention for the National Anthem. On Armistice Day, that a few tears should trickle down the cheek is not regarded as disgraceful. The display of emotion between the sexes is especially awkward.'

But surely the young have few inhibitions about such things? 'You are speaking of the sexual impulse: lack of restraint in its expression is, alas, a different matter.' Are you also saying that the English make a poor job of romantically expressing their love to each other? 'A man meets a girl and decides that he wishes to acquire her for life. In the pre-acquisition phase,' as G. put it, 'he will say a few things he will be heartily ashamed of for years. Later he will have difficulty even in saying "I love you".' Not agreeing with much of this, I asked him upon what he based his observations. 'I base them on my own observations,' he replied. 'What else? You can say that you know the human race even if you know only a sample,' he added flatly.

Do you mean there are no exceptions to the things you have been saying? After all, have you not yourself found friendship in England? 'I have.' What qualities have such friends manifested? 'Total loyalty, integrity, and violent reactions to any criticisms of me,' he said with renewed good humour. Is loyalty the best quality of a friend? 'It is often the acid test of friendship.' Is it the acid test for you?

'I think it is. Generosity also.' Have you ever been disappointed in your friends? 'Often. But not as often as I should have been had I taken a less cynical view of friendship at large.'

Are you saying that you presume, *a priori*, that friends will turn out false? 'No. My inherent assumption has always been that you cannot expect the finer qualities from every human being.' What do you expect from your friends? 'In relation to my real friends, those I have had a long time, loyalty is a sufficient test.' How many close friends could you say that you have? 'Not more than half a dozen to whom I could appeal if in need. Not necessarily material need, but moral need.' I cannot imagine, I said, that you would frequently find yourself in moral need. There was a brief silence. 'There are occasions when one is deciding whether to enlist in a particular cause, for example,' G. replied vaguely.

I asked him whether friendship, and his concerns about it, had played such a large part in his life because he had not been married. 'A marriage,' he answered, 'would only provide you with temporary support on matters of a minor scale. A wife's support at the best of times is by no means total, and it may rapidly change into hostility. The assumption must be that if it lasts long enough it will turn into hostility.' Whose assumption? I asked. 'My assumption,' he replied swiftly, an assumption which he said was based on his legal experience of divorce. But surely there are exceptions? 'Noble exceptions,' said G.; and 'many "Darby-and-Joans" to attest it,' he added. 'But terrible hostility would develop between most married couples if they were wrecked together on a desert island,' G. asserted.

It sounds to me, I remarked, as if your view of marriage has served as a deterrent in your own case. 'I was never deterred, except by the inevitable problems of who would have me and whom I would have. I came close on a number of occasions.' But you plainly do not regret not having come even closer. 'Apart from the fact that this remarkable strain of humanity to which I belong will terminate with me, I never thought it tragic,' he answered. Have you preferred the friendship of men or of women? 'I have been close to a very few men, and the same number of women.' And in them, I assume, you found loyalty? 'Loyalty, integrity, good faith, generosity and tolerance,' he said. What is loyalty? How have your 'loyal' friends behaved? 'In any situation where betrayal was possible, that was not the course they followed.'

I know that you have been frank and candid with those whom you have trusted, I said, so how did you avoid betrayal? 'I have a built-in brake, an instinctive sense of danger. There is also no one whom I would trust as a repository of certain confidences. In such matters, I am all by myself.' There are certain things that you would tell no one? 'There have always been people close to me to whom I could make revelations. But only up to a point. Certain revelations I would not make.'

This is surely true of all people, I observed. Are we not known only to ourselves, and do we not all prefer it to be so? 'Very few would admit it,' G. said. 'But one of the difficulties of life in England is that total frankness, total candour, is impossible with the English. You clash quickly with class problems, political problems and so on. In such circumstances, personal disclosure ends only in mutual embarrassment. Moreover, people are most vulnerable when they drop their guard. The British have a special interest in keeping their guard up. Who was it said, "Save me from my candid friends"? Sometimes, the candid merely hope to wound; often this is rather a vindictive world. It is rare that people will spend a whole hour praising their friends.'

Yet even if disclosure embarrasses, you must have constantly been sought out by others to hear of their personal woes. 'Yes,' G. replied, 'and I have often also been the unwilling recipient of confidences. For instance, someone came to me recently who was deeply troubled about the fact, hitherto kept from the world, that a girl with whom he was involved had been subjected to rape for a year. It was a confidence I could well have been spared.' Yes, but most people, including yourself, need to place their trust in someone? 'It is necessary for a full life to have people you trust,' G. admitted.

Is there some 'female principle' which appears to lead you to place your trust more in women than men? I asked. 'You have a softer landing with them than you do with males. If I am in terrible trouble, having said outrageous things about X, for instance, a woman would be more sympathetic, less prone to blame or to take you to task over your errors. Your women friends are more prone to sympathise.'

There are many married men who would disagree, I said, with wives who are quick to judge them as the architects of their own misfortunes. 'Ah, but wives are generally women who have been conditioned by horrible experiences over a number of years.' All wives? 'I know of marriages where the whole situation remains idyllic, but many more cases of disillusion.' You seem to have a sceptical view of the married state as such. 'That is a little too obvious as a position to take. Generalisations about marriage are ill-advised. As a lawyer I do not like divorce practice, but it is hard to escape certain conclusions from the experience of it. Marriage starts off with a blaze of friendship and trust which dies down quickly, and settles into routine. Indeed, routine often appears to be the best one can hope for after the first flames have dimmed,' he declared.

Are you claiming that it is difficult for friendship between the partners to survive marriage? 'Ordinarily,' he replied, 'friendship won't survive marriage.' You must therefore feel you have been spared. 'I have been spared the disillusionment. But one always needs companionship, and that is more easily provided by a woman than a man.' He himself had had 'four intimate relationships with women consecutively'. The first, G. said, 'was with an ATS officer in the Army. It was obvious that she had expected that I might marry her. But I hesitated, and she went off with someone else.' Did you regret that? 'I was regretful, but not for long. Then there was Anne Fleming. Our friendship was close, remarkable. She provided me with the companionship that I wanted, especially when travelling. It would not require a private detective,' he said, chuckling, 'to identify the other two.'

You told me the other day that your mother had let you know that she wouldn't have objected to your marrying a Christian. 'She said that that fact should not stop me from marrying. But she wouldn't have liked it.' And not having married, the companionship of both male and female friends becomes the more important? 'It is a necessary distraction at times, when you have to find ways of killing time,' he answered. In order to 'kill time', are you glad of the presence of male friends? 'You must be selective, or you'll find yourself irritated beyond measure.' By what? 'Their very existence, their prejudices, their habits. You must find a set of people who don't affront you.'

That sounds like a predisposition to irritation at the presence of others, I said. He shook his head. 'I have an amenable disposition and a high degree of tolerance for others. It is rare for me to be irritated in that way. I was recently lured to a dinner with utterly obnoxious people. The temptation to say something about their demeanour was powerful, but I resisted it.' But if the 'very existence' of others is a potential irritant, it suggests that you have less patience than you pretend. 'It depends on how long a time elapses before you express indignation about the irritating behaviour of others. I go out of my way not to offend people. Of course, this itself may be pure self-indulgence,' he said jocularly.

How is it that you also see companionship as a means of 'killing time'? It surprises me that you should need to 'kill time'. 'All successful life,' G. answered, 'depends on the success one has in killing time. All that you do is killing time. You read a book, you listen to the radio, you watch TV, you go for a walk – not something I do – you go for a drive. Such activities serve to make the passage of the day more tolerable.' Is life not tolerable without such activities, then? 'No, it does not mean that. They enable you to occupy yourself in a way that is distracting.' Distracting from what? 'Distracting yourself from yourself,' G. replied.

All this suggests an anxiety about the void, said I. 'Everyone has anxieties about whether his self-reliance will suffice. I never had much doubt about that. But such an attitude is itself a form of complacency. Complacency is a good quality, but it should not be too obvious to others, or you will become odious to your companions. If there were such a person as an average man,' he continued, moving further from 'the void', 'I would be slightly superior in moral terms, in social terms, in generosity. In such matters, I have a slight edge. I am better than the mass of mankind, but not better than the best of mankind. They leave me outstripped.'

You also keep certain matters at a distance, not least by humour, I said. 'Humour is a buffer.' Is friendship the opposite of loneliness? I asked. 'No. It's the opposite of . . .' G. paused. 'It is a requisite, in order to be a tolerant, normal human being.' And if the English, as you say, find friendship difficult, in that respect they must be less than 'normal' or 'human', and you more normal, and more human? 'One thing I have never pretended is that I am English. An English Jew is something very considerably different. It is silly for me to pretend that I am an Englishman. First of all, I am not a Christian. I hold Christian beliefs to be superstition.' Perhaps, I said, others have sought you out precisely because there are qualities in you which are 'not English'? 'I can't answer "no" to that. Friends are attracted to the qualities they find in one. It is quite likely that my non-English qualities make me attractive to some people.'

And you have also found friends among your professional clients? 'Some clients become friends within the hour.' How so? 'Sometimes the relationship is weighed in favour of friendship because of the urgency of their need. It is a good basis for friendship.' Are you glad of friendships made on the basis of such need? 'I am glad of the realisation that people need my support. It is a compliment that they feel I am able to supply it. And in a smaller way I can encourage their good behaviour. A lawyer can, of course, also encourage bad behaviour, greed and so on.' Is it easier, do you think, for a lawyer than a doctor to make friends with his customers? 'It is dangerous for a doctor to do so,' he answered. 'His role presupposes the giving and taking of disagreeable advice. In such circumstances, friendship is harder.'

But you have made many friends in England, close or not. There are others, English and non-English alike, who are more dismayed than you by the difficulties placed in the path of friendship in England, who come not to like the place much for that reason. 'I like England. It is safe and secure here. Here Jews are in no way passengers. In many parts of the world they regard themselves as "on approval". Here you can, of course, get the impression that the English do not much like you as a Jew. It is largely because you are different, or because they resent your pretence that you are the same. There is nothing more ridiculous, for instance, than for a Jew in a silk hat to ride on a horse in pursuit of a fox. The Englishman may come to admire such a Jew's skill, but on the whole it stands out like a sore thumb.'

Surely it is not only Jews who do not look well on horseback? 'True, the grocer and the ironmonger can also cut a poor figure chasing a fox. But I cannot see Isaiah Berlin going to a meet, or pursuing a fox over a variety of fences,' G. said, laughing. 'I would not reproach a Jew who wanted to hunt, but I would be somewhat suspicious of his motives. Nor would I condemn him, provided that he did no injury to the horse.' But it is not such Jewish pretences which stand in the way of Jews' friendships with non-Jews, I said. 'No. It is very difficult for the English to attain friendship among themselves. Such failure they often smooth over. The political friendship, for example, is a total unreality.' Why? 'Because politicians are involved in activities designed for self-aggrandisement and the diminution of the significance of their rivals.' Isn't the larger problem the lack of spontaneity in English friendship?

'The English are above all very distrustful of each other. They do not bestow confidences very readily or quickly. It is sad, because their lives are the emptier for that. It is not to say that every Englishman is incapable of a strong and genuine feeling of friendship. But it is rarer among English-men than other people. However, if the English character is not disposed to enjoy deep friendship, the compensation is that it is not aware of the defect.' This was said with a chuckle. 'The national character,' he added, 'would be richer and deeper if it was capable of such friendship.'

Do you really mean that the English in general can't be friends? 'I place the emphasis on a true friendship,' G. said. 'The numbers of English who attain a friendship which transcends shallow emotions are few.' Expressions of what G. called 'friendship on a sanitised scale' were a different matter, and commonplace. 'In Italy, people readily fall into each other's arms. They do things much more conspicuously than we do in England. This may itself be hypocrisy, but a mixture of the two attitudes [Italian and English] would be a good thing.

'Of course,' he continued, 'one must guard against making friends too easily. If within an hour of meeting a new person you fall on his neck, consider him a lifelong friend, and declare that the relationship will go on for ever, unruffled, you will be deceived.' Despite this, it is the 'emotions of friendship' by which you yourself lay great store, while suggesting that the English do not display, or do not feel, them. 'It is difficult for the English to engender enough emotion to sustain a friendship. Indeed, most Englishmen would compliment themselves on not being emotional.'

But you are not saying, are you, that the English are entirely without passion? 'They have passions for special-ised interests,' said G. 'They are passionate foxhunters. They are passionate soccer fans, to the point of homicide. But they do not rate human beings. Human beings are less important to them than other considerations.' You have suggested several times that the British are 'afraid' in some way of friendly emotion. What are they afraid of? 'They are afraid of offending the conventions,' G. answered. Does an embrace, then, or a warm handshake, offend the conventions? 'Even a warm handshake can offend the conventions. But the English also use their coldness to good effect. They have maintained the best armies in the world since such coldness is conducive to physical bravery. They do not love themselves enough to protect themselves as they might.'

Against odds like these, what kind of emotions are you trying to engender in your friends? 'I do not want to engender emotion. But particularly in the case of women, it might seem that there is insufficient emotion in their relationships. The time when there is high emotion is at the peak of courtship. At that time, the English begin to use the word "love". Afterwards, they are embarrassed by it,' he repeated. 'Neither Roland nor Oliver were English,' he added.

But how do you recognise in yourself the presence of feelings of 'true friendship'? 'When you need to be with the other person, and would be prepared to make sacrifices for him, in particular moral sacrifices, and to sustain him when there is a moral problem. I have had two friendships of this kind, which started in my schooldays. There are four or five other people who can be regarded as friends, within my definition of the term. Others are acquaintances, in which the relationship does not go beyond the safe limits of emotion.'

And when does an 'acquaintance' become a 'friend', with the capacity to arouse such emotion? 'I would be slow to analyse it,' said G. elusively. Then what does the emotion of friendship permit you to feel? 'It is an emotion which enables you, for instance, to join in ranks whose beliefs you might not otherwise approve.' What do you mean? 'A friend might entertain some belief alien to your own, but you would not, as a friend, allow it to over-shadow your friendship.'

You have criticised English reticence and reserve, but are they not in some circumstances virtues? 'I think they are,' G. answered. Even shyness? 'They are virtues, but virtues which do not relate to friendship.' Do they stand in the way of friendship? 'Yes, they do. But you can alleviate shyness by experience, particularly when you find out that you are not the principal subject of the conversation of your friends.'

You have obviously set great store by friendship, I remarked, judging by the thought you have given to it. 'True friendship is a warming relationship. It provides you with somewhere to go when you need guidance or assistance.' Are you not then self-reliant? 'No, no! No man is an island.' Do you also believe, as I do, that in England success in life, however modest, has a tendency to diminish the number of one's true friends? 'It diminishes the number of your friends for two reasons. First, success causes jealousy and gets in the way of friendship. Secondly, you yourself, when you succeed, come to see that numbers of people have attached themselves to you because of your success and for no other reason. I have had considerable experience of it.'

Despite the 'brake' which you yourself apply, have there been betrayals by false friends which have shocked you? 'I cease to be shocked at betrayal by those whom one has regarded as friends.' How have you been betrayed? 'When friends support things you do not like, for example, and know you do not like them. Or when friends have to choose between their interests and your interests, and choose their own.' Do you mean that you actually expect your friends to prefer your interests to theirs? 'It is not a bad definition of friendship.'

And friendlessness? 'To be friendless is a very sad situation. Friendship is one of the consolations for living.' Are there others? 'Food is a consolation, going to watch a cricket-match is a consolation, listening to music is a consolation. There are many; you could occupy your entire day with consolations. But in the end it would be a waste of time.' Why? Is it because an admixture of pain is required amid the pleasures? 'I think so. But no sane man would go out of his way to seek pain, or he would be paying constant visits to the dentist for the sheer fun of it,' said G. merrily.

Nevertheless, I said, pain cannot be avoided however you try, and with friends or without. 'Life has difficult periods for everyone, except for the officers of the Salvation Army. But the knowledge that there are people who would support you is a great comfort,' G. declared. You might like such people, said I, but could you say you loved them? 'That depends on the duration and the interest of the relationship, and when your inner self tells you that love exists. The essential quality of love is that it is a finite experience, although occasionally it may survive for a lifetime.'

You never thought that in marriage such love might be found? 'If society were to begin again, the whole institution of marriage would never be reconceived. It exists merely to respectabilise the sexual activities of the partners.' But are you also saying that it is easier to remain friends with someone if you don't live exclusively with him or her? 'A commitment to another person for 24 hours a day can only survive with very unselfish people.'

Were you yourself too selfish to contemplate it? 'If you are asking me why I did not marry . . .' G. jovially began.

I am not, I replied. 'Well, I'm telling you . . . first of all, it was because of the accident of time. I enlisted and spent six years in the Army. I came out of it penniless and had to take up legal practice with energy and commitment. I had little time for romance. There was also in me an underlying doubt as to whether I could have confidence in any other human being. I never had a relationship which reassured me sufficiently for me to wish it to remain an exclusive relationship for the rest of my life.'

Does this mean that, despite all you have said, you are inwardly sceptical about the possibility of lasting relationships, those of friendship included? 'No, no,' G. protested. 'But it is hard to find such people [lasting friends]. The best test is that of Captain Dreyfus. He found quite a lot of people prepared to support him, many for political reasons and only a few from honourable, personal motives. It is also difficult to know whether a person who forsakes you does so for justifiable reasons,' G. added.

Would you say that rivalry for your friendship has got in the way of relationships with certain individuals? 'That would be vain to believe,' G. answered, 'but there has certainly been rivalry between my women friends. If I have been close for a time to a particular person, invariably another woman will feel resentment even if she has exiguous claims to me.' Doesn't this rivalry flatter you? 'It is irritating, silly,' G. replied shortly.

Why does this sense of resentment afflict your women friends, and not your male friends? 'I do not think one man will deplore your relationship with another man because he is jealous. But women certainly will. They feel themselves much more endangered than men. A wife can quite reasonably consider any woman in her circle as a menace to her safety. From my limited experiences of giving matrimonial advice, one of the most nauseating is to hear a man say, "I have fallen out of love with Mary, but I have fallen in love with Edna."'

Why 'nauseating'? 'Because marriage involves some sacrifice in the delights of knowing every man or woman who is around.' To some it may represent an intolerable restraint, I said. 'It is not intolerable. It is a necessary restraint,' G. replied. Yet you found the prospect of it irksome. 'It was not irksome. I refrained because no one appeared whom I wanted to marry, or who would marry me.'

That sounds as if you had some self-doubt as to your attractiveness, or appeal, to a woman. 'It may be complacent on my part, but I have never worried about how I appear in others' eyes. That is probably a fault,' he declared. I cannot believe you have never had this anxiety. Surely all of us harbour some doubt, at some time, about the impression we make on others? 'But I was complacent enough to believe,' G. repeated, 'that such matters would not arouse disapproval in the eyes of right-thinking people. There were, however, limits even to my expectations,' he said, laughing. 'Obviously, one wants large crowds shouting, "Goodman for President!", but they did not do so.'

From what did this *amour-propre* derive? I asked him. 'From the *amour-propre* given me by the fairies at my birth,' was G.'s reply. 'Too large a quantity of it would have been a formula for unhappiness. But a small amount, such as I was given, was a recipe for happiness. It was doled out to me in the right proportion. Therefore, I had no need to go around building foundations for my *amour-propre*. Moreover, it would be priggish to be proud, say, of my intellectual success, or of my material success, in which I was not very interested in the first place. I would be prouder of my army record if I had won the VC,' he added sardonically. 'But the likelihood of that was non-existent, and apparent to everyone as soon as I put on a uniform. I would have also gone to some lengths to avoid a situation in which I could have won a VC,' G. said with great merriment.

You have several different circles of friends, do you not, many of whom do not know each other? 'I do.' Do you ever try to bring them together? 'I have no such conscious aspiration. I do not mind them coming together, but to *want* to bring people together is aping God.' Why? 'It makes the assumption that two people who do not know each other are going to like each other because you have brought them together.'

Has the friendship of the great and good, the powerful and the talented, been particularly gratifying to you? 'No,' G. replied on the instant. 'I have never enjoyed a relationship simply because I was impressed by the achievements of the person concerned. I have had friendships both with the successful and the unsuccessful Some of my closest friendships have been with completely ordinary people.' What do you mean by 'ordinary'? 'Those lacking in particular distinction, whether of intellect or anything else. But they have had something about them which attracted me, or gave me satisfaction. My closest relationship in the Army was with a little lance-bombardiet – I say little because he was physically small – with whom I retained a friendship until the end of his life. He was a person of immense virtue, industrious, who lacked any sense of ambition and died alone, but without being a recluse.' You make it seem as if you believed 'lack of ambition' to be a virtue, I said. Is it? 'Of course,' G. answered, without hesitation. 'There is nothing more odious than concealed ambition.'

What is wrong with the ambition of honour, for example?

'The ambition to be honoured is singularly odious,' he replied. 'There is nothing worse than a wife, for instance, who comes to you declaring that her husband is unaware of her visit and who then complains that he has been denied a legitimate honour.' You have had such experiences? 'Many. There are considerable numbers of people who believe that only ill luck has denied them public recognition.' But what is bad about the public recognition of one's virtues? 'The public recognition of one's virtues is not "bad". But there is a difference between gaining such recognition and going in quest of it.'

What you are saying is that people come to you seeking your aid in obtaining honours for themselves? 'Most certainly.' How many? 'In a year, four or five will come to me with requests that I should assist them to obtain some honour or other. I am always disgusted.' But if it reflects a desire to gain recognition from the world for their activities or merits, is it so reprehensible? What is so wrong with it? I repeated.

'It distorts your relationships in other directions,' G. replied. 'If you are constantly in search of recognition, you also lose time which could be better spent.' Yes, but for some people at least, such as insecure Jews, could not such recognition represent a token of their acceptance? 'The quest for honours is not confined to Jews,' G. answered. 'But some Jews may think that they have a reduced status in society, and that such honours will reduce their reduction.' Are such thoughts to be condemned? 'They are undesirable for the people themselves. Mrs Simpson's last years were devoted to acquiring the title of "Her Royal Highness". It is difficult to think of a more avid quest in the history of mankind.'

Yes, but your own activities have been crowned with such honours, said I; it could seem to some that, by pulling up the ladder, you were leaving those trying to clamber up behind you stranded. 'The numbers clambering up behind are so large,' he chuckled, 'that they would occupy all the ladders in the United Kingdom. It is also not true that I have done what you say.' But what about your own honours? 'Any honour I received was never sought,' he said good-humouredly. 'I would be sitting quietly at home and a letter would arrive from the Prime Minister offering me this or that honour. On one occasion, I was even offered a choice of honours.'

You are not saying that this displeased you? 'It was agreeable and gratifying, but the more gratifying because I had done nothing to achieve it. It would not, of course, have been discreditable had I decided that I would have liked to be a Duke. It would have been absurd, but not discreditable.' Yes, but while you make fun of some of this, others, unsung, lie in outer darkness, and some of these may be of great dignity and worth. Why should they not want notice too? 'An obsessive quest for honours is not a token of great dignity,' G. replied.

But did not your acquiring of honours give you confirmation of a certain kind? 'It did not confirm anything; only that I had succeeded in choosing a path which brought its own rewards.' He observed my quizzical expression. 'It sounds bogus and hypocritical, but honours came to me accidentally.' Do you not have sympathy for those of merit who languish in dark corners? 'Not for those who are after trivial awards because they think society owes it to them. Indeed, the nicest people I know have refused honours. My closest friend refused a knighthood.'

Were you not tempted to refuse in the same way? I asked. 'On the contrary. At the moment an honour is offered,' he replied, laughing, 'I snap it up in case the honour is withdrawn before I can take it.' I can see, said I, that your objection is not to honours as such but to the unseemly pursuit of them. 'There are great numbers of the human race who would regard themselves as having a claim on public honours, and who pine when they don't get them.' Perhaps because the public regards such honours as a token of merit, said I, and those without them as in some sense inferior. 'Charlie Chaplin was honoured when he was approaching or past 80, and no one had thought the worse of him in the years before. My opinion of the work of those who are artistically talented, for instance, would not be affected by their being given or not given an honour.'

I then enquired of him, changing the subject after this detour, whether in his friendships with non-Jews, curiosity about or interest in his being a Jew, and in Jewishness, was often manifested. 'Sometimes,' he replied. In what spirit? 'When the matter has been raised, I have had the sense of its being raised with covert hostility. On the other hand, those who love Jews – an attitude I would regard as eccentric – would generally not raise it at all, for fear of giving offence. When there is real friendship between Jews and non-Jews they can raise the subject, and you can raise it, without ulterior motivation.'

Did you find yourself discussing the matter with prime ministers, for example? What about Harold Wilson? 'He had an interest in the Jews. But it arose from the fact, rather an unhealthy fact, that Jews were the first to whom he would look for material support, and those who gave him such support did so in the belief that he would honour them. The prime ministers I was closest to were Harold Wilson and Edward Heath. The latter did not appear to have any complex about the Jews. He just regards them as part of the community. But Wilson appeared to prefer the company of Jews to any other company. Some of them,' G. added mordantly, 'were very unattractive, and others undeserving.'

Why do you think he consorted in this way with Jews? 'Because he did not belong firmly to any community of his own. He was, I suppose, essentially middle class: he had not come from the working classes. He found that Jews provided him with a society for which you needed no testimonial for admission. Jews rarely have a strong sense of class. And because they are insecure they themselves tend to go in quest of those who appear to be secure, and to boast about it. Wilson felt at ease with them, whereas he was not at all at ease with the Tory aristocracy, for example.'

Did you regard yourself as a friend of Harold Wilson? 'I regarded myself for a long time as under a duty of friendship to him; it was a duty rather than a spontaneous thing. He elevated me to the peerage. At the time, he said that the Labour Party would expect me to support it in the House of Lords if I was made a peer. This I said I could not do. Nevertheless, six weeks later he recommended me.'

Were you in general chary of close political friendships? 'Not from any principle. I was a close friend of Roy Jenkins, and a close acquaintance of Richard Crossman – nobody could have been a close friend of his.' But you have suggested to me on other occasions that you have a certain scepticism about politicians. 'Such scepticism as not to be one myself. George Wigg urged me to be a member of parliament. He offered me Bath. I decided I did not want it.' Out of antipathy for the political life? 'Out of antipathy for the beliefs which I would have had to espouse. I could not be an uncritical adherent of any party's manifesto; I would be too disposed to search out its difficulties. This may be a fault, but I would not have been able to condemn a friend who happened to be a Conservative.'

You believe in forgiving the trespasses of your friends, then? 'The essence of friendship, once it is established, is that you do not judge your friends. They have passed the test.'

Does it mean they can do anything without reproach? 'No. But they can do a good deal more than strangers.'

[3]

The Liberal

I asked G. about his political beliefs, wishing to find out what they were. At the outset he described himself as a 'conventional and unalloyed liberal', and 'really a Gladstonian liberal', even if there was 'no party manifesto which expresses those beliefs from my point of view'. 'All the things I hate – cruelty, injustice, intolerance – would have to be part of such a manifesto,' he added. But no manifesto rested sufficiently upon such premises.

And how far are you a socialist? 'I am not a socialist,' G. answered, 'but I am in sympathy with parts of socialist belief.' To what do you object about socialism? 'The ideal of equality,' he answered. 'It is impractical, and it is damaging to a society to go in quest of it. On the other hand, I am violently opposed to greed, and consider it objectionable that certain people are able to make fortunes without any form of control.'

Nevertheless, despite your great friendship for Aneurin Bevan and Jennie Lee they did not succeed in making you a socialist? 'On the contrary. But my friendship with Aneurin Bevan gave me a great admiration for him. He was essentially a fair-minded man. But if I had been a Conservative charged with a crime, I would not have wanted him on the jury.' You couldn't have been a Tory yourself? 'No, no,' G. said with alacrity. 'I couldn't have been a Tory.' Why not? 'Because of the Tories' belief in the sanctity of property. It is a simple belief which binds the Tory Party together. The Labour Party has no comparably simple belief; they have been in search of it for generations.' Are you saying that Labour and socialism are activated by no 'great idea'? 'They are activated by a complex of great ideas.' But you yourself seemed to pick out egalitarianism as a governing socialist or Labour idea? 'Only to an extent. Their spokesmen may possess a belief in it, but it is doubtful whether the rank and file do. Socialists also believe in the abolition of poverty, they believe in social service, they believe in inalienable rights, they believe in a national health service and free education. In these respects Labour is streets ahead of any other party in morality.'

Yet you never joined the Labour Party, I observed. 'I never could have joined the Labour Party.' Why not? 'Because of its marginal arguments,' he replied oddly. What do you mean? 'Arguments about the national health service, about taxation, and so on. They rarely come to agreement in the party: "pull devil, pull baker",' he added. You mean that because Labour people argue about policy, you were deterred from joining? 'I would not have been able to take part in those arguments,' he declared.

But was that a sufficient reason? 'It was one of the reasons,' he answered. 'But their manifesto never carried my full approval. Moreover, they have never issued a manifesto to which they have adhered.' So what you are saying basically is that you are mistrustful of Labour policy in one respect or another, and of the way the party conducts itself? 'Harold Wilson, for example, started off with virtuous ideas, but did not stay with them for long.'

Why do you think that was? 'He succumbed to undesirable influences which should not have weighed with any responsible man.' Such as? 'Such as Lady Falkender,' G. replied. 'He also had a penchant for associating with, and in the end honouring, rich and successful Jews. He need not have.'

Was there some fatal flaw in his belief which carried Wilson in these directions? 'No, not in his beliefs. The flaw was in himself. He was also the best illustration of the truth that anyone in public life, especially a prime minister, should be provided with a satisfactory income for his purposes. Because he was not, he was attracted by the clink of gold in the possession of undesirable people.' Are you suggesting that Labour politicians in general fail to live up to their principles? 'No. Aneurin Bevan and Jennie Lee did not fail to live up to their principles.'

I've gathered, said I, that you were unable to accept the 'line' of the Labour Party. 'I would have found it impossible to pledge myself to any party manifesto,' G. repeated. To what in particular did you demur? 'I not only demurred, but took an active part in repelling the suggestion – the worst offence – that everyone should belong to a trades union if they wished to obtain, or retain, particular employment, writers included. I also took exception to Mrs Castle's attempt to stamp out private medicine.'

Do you mean that you share the view that the trades unions are in some way Labour's incubus? 'I share my own view,' said G., 'that to be compelled to belong to any association is illiberal, dangerous and wrong. If you want a full statement of my views on this matter, read Nora Beloff's *Freedom Under Foot*. She has an idiotic objection to left-wing causes, but she has accurately set out my ideas there.'

Do you share any of the conventional objections to 'leftism'? 'I certainly thought that Tony Benn' – whom he described as 'quite a friend, he consulted me the other day' – 'took an impractical course in his political life. The problem lies in the socialist philosophy of equality,' G. again said. What is impractical about it? 'It depends upon lobbying the Almighty for something which He is not doing at the moment. Equality could be secured only by divine intervention. Since I do not believe in divine intervention, I do not believe in the possibility of equality either.'

Yet, I said, you are associated in the public mind with an instinct for the downtrodden. Shouldn't that instinct have made you a socialist? 'I don't think that socialism will secure the downtrodden to be uptrodden,' G. answered. 'There is something in the Tory complaint that Labour has the instinct to level down rather than to level up. They would rather have a community of paupers than of millionaires. I do not go for either.'

That could also be regarded, like some of your other political views, as sitting on the fence, I remarked. 'Phrases like that don't have any serious moral significance,' G. said shortly. 'Sensible people sit on the fence until the dangerous bull has gone into the next field.' But don't you think that, in order to redeem mankind, socialist types of intervention in human affairs are required? 'If I was to take a holiday,' G. obliquely replied, 'on the whole I'd prefer the company of socialists to the company of Tories. But I would rather take it with people not committed to any particular philosophy.'

Yes, but doesn't being uncommitted make it easier to trim? 'Trimming doesn't arise. "Trimming" means you are consciously departing from a specific belief which you hold, because it is safer to do so. I have never expressed any beliefs from which I could trim,' he added laughingly, joking against himself. That's like saying you have no moral commitments, which I know not to be so. 'I am not a moralist,' G. replied. 'I do not condemn people who act in a way which is contrary to my moral code. I condemn them if they act in a fashion at variance with their own moral codes, and even more if they have no moral code at all.'

That is to be a moralist, said I; and surely you and the friends whom you prefer have fixed principles, political as well as any? 'Few of my friends are committed to any particular doctrine,' G. replied. 'But on the whole, most of them would have voted Labour.' Does that signify that they are socialists, broadly speaking? 'It signifies that they find Tory positions more odious than others, and find Tories, as people, generally more odious than other people.'

Do you share their view? 'Yes.' Why? 'Because their concern for property is excessive and immoral. There is never a parliament under a Tory government which does not enact some new protection for property and property-owners.' So it is Tory addiction to property which sticks in your craw? 'Not property in the narrow sense, but their addiction to material interests.'

But surely, I said, you yourself would be against sybaritic laws, or expropriation? 'I don't want to see more legislation on any matter,' he answered, side-stepping the issue. 'There is enough legislation on the statute book to protect the individual from any ordinary kind of harm . . .' Do you really mean you don't want more legislation on any subject? '. . . Take so-called "race relations" for example. You cannot legislate for love,' G. declared. Was it on the grounds of leaving well alone that you voted against the War Crimes Bill, which provided for the prosecution of

Nazi war criminals resident in Britain? 'Partly for that reason,' G. replied. 'But the offences which the Bill sought to pursue were much too old. It is undeniable that their pursuit would now be cruel.' Not everyone thinks so. 'No doubt my opposition to it would alienate people in quest of revenge,' was G.'s brisk answer.

After hearing what you are against – Labour egalitarianism,' Tory greed, for example – I would think your liberalism a half-way house between extremes. 'I am more hostile to Tory greed. There is more virtue in egalitarianism.' But you do seem to be somewhat clearer about what you are against than what you are for, said I. 'No. I think I am for freedom of expression, liberty of thought, freedom of publication – for the great freedoms which enable people to breathe more easily.' But not for party or any party doctrine? 'I could never identify with any particular party. There is enough obscurity in party politics to make one disinclined to join any party.' Why do you single out 'obscurity' as the deterrent? 'If you strike out in favour of one party's policies you will end up not knowing what policies you are subscribing to.' You mean that you fear to be deceived? 'I resist party generalisations which, when analysed, can be seen to promise the impossible to the credulous,' G. replied.

Is it the doctrinaire, or what you have called 'fanaticism', which you are anxious to avoid? 'That is a precaution to be taken by anyone, whatever political opinion he may be weighing. Extremism is a danger to humanity.' Does this impel you, as a self-confessed liberal, towards 'the middle ground'? 'I am not anxious,' G. now said, 'to qualify as a liberal.' You told me you were. 'In saying I was a "liberal", it was merely another way of declaring a dislike of extremism,' G. replied. In party terms, then, you occupy some kind of 'no man's land'?

'It is a compliment to say one has planted a flag in no man's land,' said G., good-humour returning. 'As soon as you plant it on someone else's land you are in conflict with ownership.' Not necessarily in conflict, said I; but it really sounds as if you are declaring yourself to be 'above party'. 'I do not see myself as above anything. That is vanity. But I see no attraction in belonging to a party,' he repeated. Perhaps because it frees you to pursue the via media, I said. 'It is nothng as positive as that. Whenever I examine party manifestos, I find large elements of untruth, impracticality and unreality in them.'

Or do you discover 'impracticality' and 'untruth' in them because you believe, broadly, in 'leaving well alone'? 'One of the first lectures I gave [as a teacher in Cambridge] was an attack on the excessive amount of legislation which was being passed. I think there are too many rules, too many laws.' But are they not the product of the politician's ambition to improve the course of things? 'I am not much impressed by politicians, neither by what they do nor by what they don't do. When I am impressed, I am more impressed by what they don't do,' G. added, laughing. 'A politician is a man who has dedicated his life to telling mankind what to do, and that is little short of an impertinence. They are like stockbrokers. Society could do very well without them.'

But as to interfering politicians and legislators, you also said the other day that you wanted to see wealth 'controlled'. 'Certainly,' G. said. 'In a long life, I have observed that successful greed is a terribly destructive force. People should not be allowed to deploy their greeds uninterrupted.' Why do you feel such hostility towards greed? 'It has a great deal to answer for. It is the most corrupting element in society. Blackmail, burglary and many other types of crime are committed from greed. It is a large evil and a comprehensive word.' But why, among human sins, do you single out greed in this fashion? Why not choose envy, say? 'Envy is connected with greed,' said G. But why greed? 'I have found myself in a world,' G. replied with vehemence, 'where greed abounds and people are unashamed of it. Greed nullifies so many good things. It nullifies charity, for instance; a greedy man will give little, or disproportionately to his means. It nullifies friendship also.'

Have you always thought so ill of greed? I asked. 'My feelings about it have developed with my professional experience of it. I have seen naked greed in its worst aspects,' G. declared. In politicians too? 'Politicians suffer from a special sort of greed, a greed for power,' G. answered. But should one not distinguish between one greed and another? 'Whether a person is greedy for money or power, it is to want something with a particular intensity which the object of the greed does not deserve,' replied G.

But this 'greed' could also be seen in the way Adam Smith sees it, as an expression of aspiration for self-advancement, and as a benevolent enough emotion in its effects, which make the world go round. 'I have great respect for Adam Smith,' said G. 'But it is a simplification to say that such aspiration is a benevolent emotion or that it "makes the world go round". If it does, it makes the world go round in the wrong direction.' You have also criticised ambition to me . . . 'It is connected, it is a form of greed,' G. interjected . . . In which case, and along with other things you have said, it is as if you were more in favour of quiescence than a life of action? 'If I had to choose between a quiescent and a greedy humanity, I'd plonk for the former.'

Maybe, said I, but nothing would get done. 'I don't

think that has any meaning,' G. said. 'Things that need to be done will get done.' That sounds like Adam Smith's 'hidden hand', I observed. 'Any appetite pursued with excessive zeal does not take long to become vicious,' said G., brushing the comment aside. Your motto must be the Greek one, '*μηδεν ἀγαν*' or 'nothing to excess', said I. 'Quite. It is a splendid maxim.' Which, in general, conduces to inaction? 'It is a maxim for inaction rather than action,' G. conceded.

But I can't believe that you are against an energetic life *per se*, when your own life has been as it is? 'What I have said does not refer to an energetic life,' G. replied. 'If you spent your life in cutting down trees, like Gladstone, that would not be an injurious proclivity.' It is a Thatcherite world of material self-seeking to which you most object? 'The world of Mrs Thatcher was to my view abhorrent. By and large she was an honourable and single-minded lady. But her politics and philosophy I found unacceptable. For individuals to get their hands on as much as possible showed a worthy ambition from her point of view.' Yet, said I, you cannot really excoriate ambition as such. 'Ambition must fall within a recognised limit,' said G.

In which case, the legislator must also act against excess. 'I am not sure that you have to act against anything,' said G. stubbornly. 'You have to begin by teaching people what is right. It is better to begin by teaching rather than by action.' Yet our education system is increasingly failing to teach anything, let alone the moral principles you profess. 'If teaching is failing, then action will also fail in the long run.' That is tantamount to saying you can do nothing about anything. 'That may be the best thing,' G. declared. A philosophy of 'masterly inactivity'? 'That is decorating the word "inactivity" with an adjective it does not deserve,' G. rejoined with some asperity. There was a brief silence. 'My principles would lead in more situations to inactivity than activity', he repeated.

I imagine, then, that such things as 'socialist controls' you would be against? 'I do not dislike them because they're socialist. I do not like controls. If they do not indicate benefit for mankind, they should not exist.' Does a doctrine like 'social justice' leave you cold? 'It leaves me unimpressed until the term is etched out in fuller detail. Until then, it remains a by-word, or tag.' But do you actually think that social justice, like equality, is best not pursued at all because impossible of attainment? 'Equality is certainly impossible of attainment. Its pursuit would imply that everyone is entitled to play for Arsenal.'

So some people are less equal than others? 'I am convinced of it. I do not believe people are equal in terms of their capacities and attainments. They are equal only in respect of the initial rights with which they set off in this world.' But do you also believe that unequal people should be treated unequally? 'You have to compensate for their inequality by your behaviour towards them. You try to adjust to disparity by the way you treat people.' But not to the lengths of actively pursuing egalitarianism, or social justice, by acts of economic redistribution, for example?

'In practice,' G. answered – somewhat wearily – 'the Almighty will look after this. People with exceptional ability will gravitate towards certain positions. You cannot control this process by legislation.' But if you are opposed to the pursuit of egalitarianism, are you also opposed to privilege? 'You speak in catch-phrases. "Privilege" connotes something wrong. There may be every justification for it. To award a prize for attainment is no "privilege" in the sense you mean.' I was thinking rather of monarchy and aristocracy, said I. Do they offend you in any way? 'They don't offend my principles,' G. replied. 'In a civilised society they have to be regulated. But one of the least odious of human actions is to bestow benefits on people who have emerged from a better background than others.' Merely by accident of birth? 'By accident of birth or by some other chance that has befallen them.'

So is the House of Lords, as it is presently constituted, an adornment of our civic society in your eyes? 'It is a special facility,' G. answered, choosing his words carefully, 'which exists for rather important social reasons. It is a place where certain people are usefully employed in regulating legislation. Moreover,' G. continued, his mood lightening, 'the right to occupy a seat in the House of Lords is not necessarily a boon. It can involve terrible tedium and the agony of listening to your fellow peers orating without control.'

Hierarchy and rank, of this and other kinds do not offend you? 'They are an anomaly and an archaism, but they are not an affront. I do not think that difference in rank is all that important. It comes about ordinarily in savage societies also. A cannibal king might be appointed because he had a superior palate,' G. joked. When you have advised monarchs and princes, have you done so with the preservation of the monarchy in mind? I asked. 'When I have advised anyone it has been with the same objective: to lead them along the right course, whether they were monarchs and princes or window-cleaners. I have advised window-cleaners that it was very unwise of them to climb to the twelfth floor without some support, and monarchs not to act in a way that would enrage the multitude. It is the easiest way for them to lose their heads,' he added wryly.

But 'royalty' is a mere adornment, not a power; regicide hardly comes into it now, said I. 'Whatever they may be, monarchs and princes claim a superior status by right.

Those who claim such a status expose themselves to a considerable risk of being dethroned. I am talking of monarchs at large. If you have an established monarch it is difficult to know whether he is there as an adornment or as an established power, but he will need both [that is both to be an adornment and to have power] if he is to be successful as a monarch.' Do you detect a tendency to tear down monarchy as to tear down other institutions? I asked. 'There is a tendency to tear down anything which is regarded as established,' G. replied. 'The anarchist has come into his own,' he added.

Is this the Burkean conservative in you, who would regard it as prima facie wrong to overthrow established institutions? 'I am quite sure that there are many institutions which should be left alone, the MCC among them,' G. replied, levity returning. 'But the Inns of Court, the Courts themselves, and everything connected with the administration of the law should be altered with all speed. Look,' G. exclaimed, 'at the attitudes of the judiciary and the Bar to the abolition of wigs and gowns. No sensible person who considered the matter of wigs and gowns could fail to appreciate the objections to their existence.' But on what principles, I interrupted, do you advocate the defence and maintenance of some institutions and the radical reform of others? 'Only on the basis of the most arrogant of all elements, my judgment,' G. declared jovially. 'On the basis of my judgment,' he continued, laughing, 'I would unhesitatingly nominate institutions which should be changed, and – with more hesitation – institutions which should not be changed.' Does sentiment play a part in the choice? I asked him. 'I do not know what you mean by sentiment,' G. replied swiftly. A romantic nostalgia for things you have known or with which you are familiar, I said. 'I would be reluctant to admit that I am more prone to such a thing than are others,' G. remarked.

But you would agree, wouldn't you, that in many respects you are a traditionalist as to the values and institutions you hold dear?

'In some respects, yes. I hold dear the National Gallery, for example, and would not like to see it pulled down,' he said playfully. 'I do not hold dear the Law Courts, and would like to see them pulled down. I hold the London Zoo dear also,' he added. Despite the evident melancholy of the higher apes incarcerated there? 'I have few friends among the higher apes,' G. jokingly replied, 'and no ape at London Zoo which communicates with me on a confidential basis. But I have not detected melancholy among them.'

Their life in the zoo doesn't appear to me to be particularly happy, said I. 'I would need some persuading of this,' said G., persisting with his sardonic vein. 'They are fed regularly, receive medical attention, and are required to take exercise. All in all an ape's life is by no means an undesirable one.' How you do know? 'No ape has told me that,' G. replied, eyes twinkling. 'It is entirely surmise, and could be wholly erroneous. In the next world, I may encounter a deputation of outraged apes anxious to visit their wrath upon me.'

But if some institutions are more or less sacred, and others ripe for amendment, what about the principle of nation itself? You once told me that 'my country right or wrong' offends you. 'Any institution which is not regulated by right-thinking minds, or which invites us to believe that its claims should go unquestioned, is undesirable.' But as far as nation is concerned, is unquestioning patriotic loyalty to it impossible for you as a Jew? After all, you have told me that you are 'not an Englishman'.

'The fact that I am a Jew has nothing to do with it,' G. answered. 'My culture is English, my education was English, I was born in England and I have lived all my life in England, but I do not think I have been captured by English prejudices.' Would it have been a sorry fate if you had? 'Not a sorry fate. It is a sorry fate that a fair-thinking person should be compelled to certain decisions because they are in the atmosphere,' he continued. You mean, compelled by others' unconsidered zeal, nationalist zeal included? 'Military zeal, medical zeal or any other zeal which is not controlled by rational considerations.' But I have heard you say that rational means cannot persuade the irrational. 'I believe that the irrational cannot be persuaded by rational means. If they could, they would not be irrational,' G. chuckled.

Can a Jew have a nation, or does he carry his nation about inside him? I asked. 'He can be a loyal member of the society to which he belongs, whatever it may be. Common sense will persuade him without argument to be loyal. It is an anti-semitic notion that the Jew cannot be truly loyal because he has other loyalties too. When the necessity arises, he will rush to the colours. The irony is that he will rush to the colours on both sides, even if, in general, Jews are more selective in their enthusiasm than many others.'

Are you saying that Jews are immune from some forms of unreason? 'In general, the Jews are sceptical of excessive enthusiasm of any kind,' G. averred. 'I do not mean by that that they are sceptical about justice, for example. Such scepticism would be unworthy. But any Jew who believed in "my country, right or wrong" would also have to believe in "every Jew, right or wrong". Looking around him, he would see how foolish such a belief was.' Yet, despite what you say, Jews are not immune from fanaticism themselves.

'On the contrary. They are as prone to fanaticism as any other community. Indeed, their religion lends itself to fanaticism. Who but a fanatic,' G. asked, 'would observe a religion which required you to keep your head covered at all times and in all climates, or which forbade such a wide variety of delicious foodstuffs?'

In which case, Jewish immunity from other forms of zeal, if such immunity exists, is a paradox? 'You have certainly to exclude from their immunity from zeal whatever they believe is a matter of pure faith. Some of it may be pure nonsense,' G. gloomily added. But even if some of their faith is 'nonsense', the Jew can nevertheless arrive at distinctions between the rational and irrational as well as any other, and perhaps better than most, said I. 'The rational and irrational rub shoulders every moment of the day, whether you are a Jew or not. There are also special problems associated with being a Jew which are not common to the rest of mankind. It is very difficult, above all, to justify rationally that we are a "chosen" people. The sensible might rightly ask, "Who chose you?" Being "chosen" is a special sort of condition. But it saves quite a lot of people from the sin of pride,' G. said with a laugh.

Whether 'chosen' or not, and however 'particular' a people, would you say that the Jews frequently attain a universality of vision? 'Some do – the Spinozas and the Einsteins – by God's gift of mind.' And are the rest handicapped by the pettinesses of their faith? 'There is a lot about life, and not Jewish life alone, which conduces to pettiness,' G. replied. I said that I had been brought up to a mass of taboos. 'Your father,' G. declared, having read (and reviewed) my book *A Doctor's Life*, 'was a very intelligent, educated man. But somehow he had not the force of character to emancipate himself from the beliefs of his community.' Perhaps so, said I, taken aback by the

52

directness of his judgment. But there are also those who would say that such 'emancipation' is the root of all evil, and that the 'beliefs of the community' need to be sustained?

'Some Jews undoubtedly think it is wrong to free themselves from such beliefs and taboos. But it is not a desirable conclusion to come to,' G. replied. Are you saying it because you believe that you have yourself risen above these particularities of faith? 'I have not "risen above" them. As I have schooled myself to a particular regimen of diet, so I have schooled myself to a particular regimen of thought.' Why? 'Because it is easy otherwise to get immersed in a sea of prejudice,' G. replied; the sea in which my own father near-drowned.

Is it easy? 'Yes,' said G. bluntly. You mean, said I, that to be steeped too deep in Jewish ways is to predispose to prejudice about non-Jews, to have prejudice lurking at your elbow? 'Yes.' But you are immune from it? 'Prejudice is so manifest in society that it would be vanity to think oneself immune from it.' Then prejudice of the kind to which you have referred accompanies you too? 'It accompanies all of us.' Is there any particular prejudice to which you feel prone? 'I would hope to relate to particular individuals as individuals,' G. replied. That is, you lack the general prejudice to which we have referred. 'I am not exposed to any general prejudice,' G. said. That is to have reached an Olympian condition, said I. 'It is not Olympian. It is a rational position. I would like to bet that I do not hate anyone,' G. added. No one? What about 'odious' people, as you have called them? 'I would have hated Hitler, Goering, Goebbels, Ribbentrop and the whole lot of them,' he replied, jovially brushing aside the contradiction.

All your sagacity and dislike of impractical excess

suggests someone who is suspicious of utopias, and has a preference for the attainable, that which is within reach. 'The word "utopia" carries within it an element of doubt. To me, it suggests a dream-world. Some of the great misfortunes of the world have arisen from the belief in utopias.' Do you include the Jewish utopias of Christ and Marx? 'I disbelieve in the Christian utopia. It is based on extreme superstition. I do not believe Christ "rose from the dead"; I do not believe Christ was the Son of God,' G. again said. 'I do not think anyone is the Son of God. For its part, the Marxian utopia makes a spurious appeal to reason.'

Is it an accident that both utopias derive from the thoughts of Jews? 'It is an accident,' G. replied, 'that what turned out to be the most potent of forces [Christianity and Marxism] were inspired by Jews.' But do you think that there is a propensity in Jews to dream of other ways of living than those in which they actually live? 'Fantasies of what might redeem them cannot reasonably be thought of by the Jews of America or Britain.' Why not? 'Because in relation to the conditions under which the Jews actually live in those countries, to wish for other ways of living would be a pessimist's aspiration.'

But is all Jewish pessimism unwarranted? 'The situation of the Jews was changed by the Holocaust. A real threat is in their sights all the time. In the light of such an enormity it is very difficult to suggest to Jews that they should dismiss it from their thoughts. Who could have believed that a civilised people like the Germans would murder millions? Not many Jews wake up screaming over the horrors of the Holocaust, but they ought to. That the West could descend to such a depth of cruelty is beyond belief. But what happened once could happen again. In the capacity to dream of Hell, and to envisage it, is the reverse of utopia. It is foolish and complacent to dismiss the possibility of it; just as it is unreasonable to have it in the front of our minds, as if our neighbours at any time of the day or night could seize us and put us in gas chambers. But it cannot be excluded entirely, since there was ample public support for it. I hope – it is a fanciful hope – that there is a hell, and that in that hell Hitler is roasting on a spit. I do not think I would mind if Robert Maxwell were in the same condition.'

Do you think Maxwell has inflamed feeling against the Jews? 'What is surprising is the limited extent to which non-Jews associate him with the Jews,' G. replied. 'They see him as a picaresque character. If they think of him at all, it is as a born villain.' It is a good job that people do think of him in this way, if they do. 'It is also fair. If one is to assess the evil that Jews have done one must also assess the good. You and I would believe the balance is very largely in favour of the good. No anti-semite would think so, but neither you nor I are anti-semites. It would be very strange if we were.'

Against (Most) Doctors

G. had told me at our last meeting that he wanted to speak about doctors. So I asked him how he regarded '*mens sana in corpore sano*' as a motto-for-life. 'As a principle, it has a general validity,' G. replied, 'but there are exceptional cases where it has no validity at all. The supposition that because a person is in perfect health physically he is in perfect mental health also is unmitigated nonsense. There are many lunatics,' G. added, 'who will respond to a physical test very well.'

Would you personally think a mind might function better in a sylph-like body which had been exercised and jogged into lissom condition? 'Dr Johnson said that the mind feels its vacuity least when it is in motion, and that is a proposition I agree with.' That may be, but do mental energy and the sedentary state go happily together? 'We know too little of the human mind,' said G., 'to submit to any general propositions of that kind.'

Have you during your life paid much attention to your physical well-being? 'I have not been obsessed by it. But I also have had available to me what is not available to the average citizen: the advice of relatively sensible doctors, advice in which I could have confidence.' (This he also called 'good fortune'.) You are implying that the average citizen does not have access to sensible doctors in whom he can have confidence. 'There is a tendency in most of us to want to believe in the miraculous. This tendency is the basis of much uncritical trust in doctors.' But are you also saying that much confidence in doctors is misplaced? 'Indeed. When I employ a doctor – or rather, the doctors employ me – I myself am generally prepared to attribute to him certain qualities which, on closer examination, he may turn out not to possess. The assumption that when a man qualifies as a doctor he must also be an *intelligent* man is often false.'

You must have come across intelligent doctors, too? 'Indeed, I have. But the majority of doctors I have encountered are, by any standard, unintelligent.' That is a harsh judgment, I said; my own father was a doctor. 'One has to ask,' G. continued, 'what impels a man to a medical career. It is not his intelligence which governs his choice. In the case especially of Jewish doctors, it is parents who are inclined to advise their sons to become doctors out of a desire for their security. Most Jews,' G. added, 'have their bags packed, metaphorically speaking, and a medical degree is a highly portable qualification.'

Is this the principal explanation, in your judgment, for the existence of relatively large numbers of Jewish doctors in most societies? 'It is one of the explanations. Medicine is also a respected profession, and by being a doctor a Jew can earn a certain respect. Even if there are many unintelligent doctors, it is not possible for clearly lesser intellects – the great majority of *goyim*, if I may use the word – to qualify as doctors. It is possible for a greater proportion of Jews to qualify, and this also helps to explain their large numbers in the medical profession.'

Your thesis rests on the bold assumption that a greater proportion of Jews is intelligent than non-Jews. 'It is unarguable,' G. replied, unabashed. 'That is not to say that all Jews are more intelligent than the average, or that you cannot be intelligent if you are not a Jew. Some of the greatest idiots in the world are Jews. When I hear a Jew enunciating Thatcherite doctrines, for example, I would cheerfully send for a psychiatrist to certify him,' he added.

So, according to you, Jews gravitate towards medicine in the search for security and respect? 'They also recognise that the scales are more heavily weighted against them in other professions.' Are you then saying that the 'scientific temper', for instance, is not generally a factor in their choices? 'Einstein was a Jew, and that fact had more than an accidental consequence in relation to his intellectual stature. But the average Jewish medical man is not an Einstein.' You're surely not arguing that scientific rationalists are not to be found among Jewish doctors? 'You are extremely unlikely to find a Jewish doctor without an ounce of scientific wisdom in his head,' G. replied, 'but scientific rationalism is too elevated a term.' You'd prefer to attribute Jewish medical achievement to ambitious Jewish mothers? 'There are no realistic Jewish mothers who are unaware that medicine is one of the few professions – the law is another – where their sons can compete on equal terms with non-Jews.'

The logic of your argument so far suggests that, among the unintelligent mass of medical practitioners, Jewish doctors are generally more intelligent, or less unintelligent, than the rest? 'I have run into very many stupid doctors,' G. replied, 'very few of whom were Jewish. I have known one very stupid doctor in particular who touched the heights of stupidity. He was a very respectable, church-going, elderly gentile who failed to identify lung cancer in my mother.' Was it this early experience which coloured

58

your jaundiced view of the medical profession as a whole? 'Certainly,' said G. 'And other experiences, relatively few in number, of imbecility of a similar kind.'

Nevertheless, said I, I am surprised by your vehemence. 'My judgments are also coloured by experience of the medical profession in a political context. When doctors went on strike, I told BUPA, for instance, that I could no longer act for them. They had asked me how they could get their "rights". I replied that they could "get their rights" by enjoying sufficient respect with the public for their rights to be ceded to them.'

But despite all this, surely you must retain some healthy regard, if that is not the wrong phrase, for their skills, their dedication and so on? 'Certainly,' G. agreed, 'my own doctor in Oxford is an especially skilful and sensible man. I would abide by his judgment on any medical matter.' And you are a sort of doctor yourself, constantly taking the pulses of your anxious clients? 'I am,' said G. with gusto. 'But my only professional medical qualification is as an honorary fellow of the Royal College of Psychiatrists. When I received the honour, I gave them a solemn undertaking that I would not practise,' G. added, laughing.

Nevertheless, as a lawyer you must act the psychologist. 'It is rare that I have a client to whom it is unnecessary to administer psychological advice,' G. replied. 'Most are responsive. The hardest cases are those who come to me with a resolute determination to do injustice in the writing of their wills. I have often to try to persuade them out of it.' I expect that you have often to soothe the fevered brows of clients ill with worry. 'My belief is that if a client is worried, no one else need worry for him. There will be enough worry about without adding to it. If a man is going to be hanged in the morning,' G. chuckled, 'he will provide all the worry that is needed. A worried adviser is a bad adviser.'

Is that also the secret of your 'bedside manner'? 'I think I have the capacity, to some limited extent, of persuading people out of unreason,' G. answered obliquely. 'It is a rare gift which I deploy. Barely a week passes when I do not encounter unreason. In matrimonial matters, for instance, it is unusual that a spouse does not become thoroughly unreasonable.' Perhaps you would have preferred to be a doctor? 'No,' said G. flatly. 'I could not, in any case, have passed the examinations. You have to be adept in physics and chemistry, both of which I detest. I loathe all scientific subjects. They are alien to my thought.'

Yes, but surely you think systematically and logically, and, in that sense at least, scientifically too? 'I am a humanist,' said G., 'and unashamedly so. If I had my way, scientists would be expelled from all places of learning.' That, said I, I take with a very large pinch of salt. 'Yes,' said G., merrily. If Jews become either doctors or lawyers, was it then your lack of aptitude for scientific subjects which made you a lawyer? 'I did not want to be a doctor since medicine involved the application of scientific principles for which I had no sympathy,' G. answered. But doctors are humanists, too, I persisted; indeed, they must be humanists if they are to be good doctors.

'There are very few,' was G.'s reply. 'It is rare to find the kind of doctor to whom you are referring. As far as British doctors at least are concerned, they possess less humane qualities of the kind you mean than the common denominator of humanity.' This, said I, is a severe reproach. 'If they did possess such qualities,' G. continued, undeterred, 'they would be subjected daily to emotional outbreaks which they could not stand. Where you have to tell a wife, for example, that a loving husband will be dead within a fortnight, special powers are called for.'

And you are saying that the generality of British doctors do not possess such powers? 'They are not distinguished for the quality of their moral concerns. These concerns are not very noticeable in the medical world.' I declared to G. that his account did not in the least fit what I had observed of my father's concerns and medical knowledge. 'Obviously,' replied G., 'you have a biased view. You are right to admire your father. He was an outstanding doctor, and everyone I know who knew him recognised it. But you cannot regard him as typical. Indeed, he did not regard himself as typical, and with justice.'

No, you are right, I said; he considered himself to be a most distinctive figure, both as a man and as a doctor. But quite apart from such personal considerations, I told G., the medical profession as a whole might be outraged at your account of its defects. 'I recognise that in talking to you as I am, I run the risk of arousing general outrage, and this I will face with courage,' G. said sardonically. Nevertheless, you yourself have occasionally met with wise and humane doctors? 'Dr Fowler of Oxford is a case, and Lord Walton. But they are both men who have got to the top of their profession largely by concealing their real emotions.'

Do you mean that they have had to suppress their humane feelings for their patients? 'No, they have had to suppress their general disbelief in the truth of most scientific propositions,' G. insisted. Are you saying that they doubt the truth of their own medical knowledge? 'There is no scientific truth which is not sooner or later overturned by further knowledge,' G. replied. Does anyone doubt that the consumption of salt raises the blood pressure? I asked. 'I do not know,' said G. perversely. 'But take the belief that eating white sugar is injurious. I have great faith in John Yudkin, who enunciates this notion. But it in turn arouses opposition from corrupt doctors who are part of the sugar lobby.'

In addition to the unintelligent, we now have the 'corrupt' doctor also: you are taking a harsh view of the medical profession. 'Today, the relation between patient and doctor,' G. continued without concern, 'has been further corrupted by the NHS reforms. The health service was an enormous boon because it excluded the financial aspect from the relationship between doctor and patient. This relationship is increasingly determined by financial considerations. No general practitioner with his own budget would now prescribe psychiatric treatment under the NHS; the cost would be excessive. The "NHS" must now be regarded as in large part fraudulent. The reforms are further exposing the fallibility of many practitioners' medical knowledge. I despair for the average patient. Before, everything was referred to hospital. Now, a cash element has been injected into it, old relationships have been made enormously complicated, and its whole basis rendered suspect. Treatment,' declared G., 'should be provided free. The poor patient should not take second place to the rich, nor the cheap treatment be given precedence over the expensive.' And what about your 'unintelligent' doctor? What can be done with him? 'If you have a stupid doctor, you must make the best of it. The situation cannot be remedied immediately, unless he is so stupid that he is unaware of the efficacy of aspirin for a headache. If he is at least capable of taking a blood pressure, or prescribing for a stomach-ache or diarrhoea, he has a useful presence. But if he is incapable of diagnosing an obscure ailment, that is to be expected in the average doctor.'

What is a 'good doctor' to you? 'In my estimation, it is a caring doctor.' But you would be contradicting yourself if you were now to say that it did not matter how much a doctor knew, provided that he 'cared'. 'No, it would not necessarily be a contradiction. If he cared, he would find out rather than relying on his own ignorance. I recall being unwell on holiday in some seaside town. A young doctor appeared, and asked me "How are you today?" I thought that if I did not tell him, he would never find out.' But despite the severity of your judgments, you have not been short of expert medical advice. 'I have always had available to me a good supply of doctors, Sir Richard Bayliss, Sir John Badenoch and others.' They were a bit more than merely 'caring', were they not? 'Caring is an essential requirement. If an ordinary doctor is caring, he will find out everything that is necessary, and will rely on his own judgment rather than referring everything to hospitals and specialist opinion. I prefer a doctor to rely in the first instance on his own informed judgment.'

Yet, by your argument, there is not only relatively little reliable medical information to be found from most doctors, but you do not appear to admit that to be a doctor, and to heal the sick, is to carry out an ennobling duty to one's fellows. 'No, I do not. If a man proceeds on the basis that his activities are ennobling, he will be quite useless as an ordinary citizen. To be a doctor is not ennobling. Moreover, human practices which are "ennobling" are generally corrupt, like Mother Teresa's. It is a hard thing to say, because of the regard in which she is held, but her creation of faith-in-herself is very damaging.'

Do you see doctors in a similarly unattractive light? 'I do not see them in any special light. I see some doctors doing their work well and others in perfunctory fashion. Many proceed by conveying the impression that they possess scientific knowledge, often a fraudulent impression. Moreover, there is something wrong with a profession which cloaks itself in a spurious infallibility, an infallibility which is supposedly gained as soon as a medical student qualifies as a doctor. The same is true of the legal profession, the architectural profession and so forth. It is true of all professions. When you go to see a lawyer, you should leave your own judgment outside the consulting room.'

The client and the patient then cannot win, I said; their own knowledge is insufficient, and they will as likely as not be duped by their professional advisers? 'On the whole,' G. replied immovably, 'the lawyer is a more hopeless case than the doctor. It is merely a superstructure of convention which dictates his judgments.' Is this true, according to you, of doctors too? 'Yes, but less so. Doctors at least do not have to go about in wigs and gowns and medieval costume.' Are you suggesting that 'professionalism' is mere voodoo? 'That is another matter. I am speaking now of convention. It is said that the judge must wear a wig and gown in order to "enhance the anonymity" of his function. Yet there is no profession where anonymity is less sought than among the British judiciary. Judgments are delivered with the personal pronoun: "I hold", "I believe" and so on. In the United States judgments are more properly given in the name of the court.'

It seems that you have a particular animus against professional arrogance? Is it the claim to infallibility which mainly sticks in your gullet? 'Yes,' G. replied, 'and in whatever profession the claim is made. It is worst of all in clerics, with their claim that the Almighty is at their elbow, putting ideas into their heads.' But a belief on the part of patients in the infallibility of a doctor, for instance, may have a beneficent psychological effect, I said; it could assist in their cure. 'It may also assist in their demise,' G. rejoined.

Are you actually afraid of doctors? 'No, I am not afraid of them. I have had a perfectly executed prostate operation under Bayliss' supervision. I am now in the charge of a professor of vascular surgery, and inject myself each morning with Heparin.' That must require some stoicism, I said. 'No, only a needle with a sharp point.'

You have not had doctors as friends? 'Only in the RAMC during the war.' Are you particularly allergic to them as friends? 'Successful doctors are excessively ambitious,' G. replied. 'I can think of one, for example, whose obsession is to get a knighthood. He looks upon me as someone who can help. That kind of slanted friendship is not very healthy.' But not all doctors are after knighthoods? 'It is surprising how many are,' G. replied with a laugh. 'Jews particularly seek it, because they want the recognition as an antidote to prejudice.' Can Jewish doctors not make their way in their profession without such honours? 'They can now. Among the upper classes, however, the sentiment that "I wouldn't have Dr Cohen, he's Jewish" is still alive.

But what about those Jewish doctors who, historically, have been prominent in the courts of the great and the good? 'In general it is the worst doctors who have been consulted by the great and the good. To consult such doctors was generally to sign your own death-warrant. Sir David Davies, for example, presided over many deaths among the great and the good – George the Sixth, Lord Beaverbrook and many others. He looked after large numbers of distinguished people, most of whom expired in his hands,' said G., laughing.

All these doctors whom you excoriate, I protested, have also healed the halt and the lame. 'They have contributed to doing so. But, in many instances, the best contribution doctors could make to the health of their patients is inaction.' Yet you yourself have suffered from such inaction, said I. 'If a doctor leaves most of his patients alone long enough, they will expire or get better of their own accord,' G. returned, jocularly brushing the argument aside. There is too much levity in these judgments of yours, said I.

'One must retain a certain amount of levity on this subject, in which there is so much that is inexplicable,' said G. 'Why, for instance, should a man retain the services of a doctor whose knowledge is insufficient, and who treats diseases which he himself does not understand? It can only be judged with humour.'

[5]

Money: Its Uses and Abuses

Do you regard money with liking, unconcern, or disdain? I asked G. 'To regard it with disdain,' he said, 'would be as sensible as regarding food with disdain. Money, like food, is an essential commodity to keep yourself alive. It should not be worshipped, however, just as food should not be worshipped.' Nor, I take it, should it be regarded as the root of all evil? 'It is the root of a great deal of evil, and notably of greed, the unhappiest of human conditions.' Nevertheless, to call it 'filthy lucre', say, would be to go too far?

'You do not have to use opprobrious terms about it. Money is essential like earth, air or water. But if people go questing for it as if it were a magic commodity, that is wrong, just as is miserliness on the part of those with enough money not to need to be misers. The trouble with money is its tendency to displace all human values, values of truth, of beauty, of friendship and so on.' Hence, said I, there are various grounds for not treating it with unconcern, or lordly disdain? 'It depends on your position. If you are supplied with modest amounts of it adequate for your needs, there is no reason why you should not have an entirely objective attitude to money, undisturbed by greed or avarice. If, however, an individual is short of money, he is likely to manifest a considerable preoccupation with it.'

But those with money are generally no less anxious about it, said I. 'I have certainly never known anyone greedy for money who was totally happy, to the extent that anyone can be totally happy,' said G. 'There is also nothing more disagreeable than seeing signs of miserliness about money in people you like,' he added. What causes it? I asked. 'It is normally brought about by the individual's background and the philosophy of the home. It is a paradox. If a person had a father seized with the vice of meanness, you would think he would not inherit it. Normally, it is not so.' What is meanness? 'Meanness is a vice which derives from the belief that saving every penny is vital to a civilised form of life,' G. replied.

'Nevertheless,' he continued, 'the axiom "easy come, easy go" is also totally true. Associated with it is a phenomenon which one needs to observe. It is the grip that the spending of money holds upon some people. The rather imprecise postulation that money "burns a hole in the pocket" has a great deal of truth about it. For a thankfully limited number of people the question of how to spend money is a real problem. If you are to manage money well, there are various technical matters which need to be mastered: an important one is to know how to give it away. The Jews are extremely liberal on this question. They are also not over-selective about the objects of such liberality.'

But, in your case, I have gathered that you never felt wholly secure about money. 'That is not so,' G. now said; 'I never felt any anxiety about my livelihood.' Did you not become a solicitor because it offered good financial prospects, at a time when you have told me that you had no money? 'No. There is something wrong if a person chooses a career solely for the financial safety it might offer. You would set off on the wrong track if it was with the thought that this or that career would bring you £30,000 per annum. Today, alas, material considerations are being dangled before people more than hitherto. When legal scouts go to Oxford colleges in the search for recruits one of the major arguments they put forward is the financial safety of a legal career.'

I said that Edward Gibbon in his *Memoirs* declares that 'few men, without the spur of necessity, have the resolution to force their way through the thorns and thickets of that gloomy labyrinth,' meaning the law. And having other means to live by, Gibbon resisted his step-mother's advice to become a lawyer. 'There is an argument there,' said G. 'If you had enough to live on by other means, you would go to the law only for its intrinsic attractions. Those attractions are not as intrinsic as they ought to be.' In which case there is some truth in suggesting that the financial rewards are a compensation for the law's drudgery? 'The financial rewards are incidental. Any individual contemplating the law as a career would be deterred by the financial rewards, not encouraged.'

But is it Gibbon's 'gloomy labyrinth'? 'It can be quite exciting,' G. replied. 'But it depends on what you mean by a lawyer. I do not regard a conveyancer as a lawyer. If a man is a real lawyer, he does not regard the law as a labyrinth from which he cannot find a way out.' To you, then, it is not a dismal science and its experts are not drudges? 'To be a lawyer is essentially a middle-class qualification, and the middle class is the least interesting of the classes,' was G.'s oblique reply.

I remember many Jewish lawyers from my Manchester Jewish upbringing, I said; most of them my father regarded as shady, at least to some degree. 'A place like Manchester would have had a wide spread of Jews of all types of morality. It is quite likely that a good proportion of the lawyers would have been concerned with dubious financial transactions,' G. declared. 'But it must be said that lawyers rarely embezzle their clients' funds,' he cheerfully added, 'at least it is not as widespread as is sometimes imagined.' Nevertheless, said I, the respected grandees of the bench are one thing and the rank-and-file of solicitors another; the latter are not generally held by the man in the street to be paragons of virtue. 'The bulk of the rank-and-file is middle class,' G. repeated. 'They carry with them a respectable built-in morality. Indeed, it is sometimes rather priggish.'

But would you not concede that the popular view of the solicitor is of someone with access, as a result of their calling, to lucrative sources of wealth. 'It is a mistaken view,' said G. 'And insofar as it has truth, their "access", as you put it, to material funds is due to the fact that the rich have need of their services. Some lawyers are no doubt less avid to deal with the problems of the poor than of the rich. But many also act without thought of reward, although not the majority of them perhaps.'

Nevertheless, the fees demanded by the leaders of the Bar, for instance, suggest a notable degree of acquisitiveness, not to say of the greed you abhor. 'No, no,' G. protested. 'Those at the top of the profession will naturally make the charges which they think appropriate to their professional skills. Deploying talents of extreme rarity, they cannot be blamed for it. Moreover, it is rare for a lawyer to refuse someone who is in need of legal representation from financial considerations.'

For all that, said I, the unacquisitive lawyer is not an entirely familiar figure. Do you not possess the phrenologist's bump of acquisitiveness yourself? 'I have never got any particular pleasure from acquiring wealth, because I have not acquired it in any significant measure. I am not a rich man, even if I am thought to be so. I have never bothered about becoming a rich man. I am, however, assured that my modest three meals a day – or not so modest – will be paid for in ready cash.'

But your possessions surely please you, quite apart from having the means for three meals a day? 'By the standards of tycoonery, they are very sparse. I have not enough money to possess a yacht or the other attributes of great wealth,' G. said with merriment. 'If I had them, they would be an embarrassment to me. I do not in the least hanker after the display of wealth. A client of mine once came here and told me to look out of the window. He directed my gaze to a spanking new Bentley. "That," he said, "is for you." "No, I can't take it," I told him. "I am Chairman of the Housing Corporation, and for me to arrive at a housing estate in a Bentley would arouse critical and adverse comment, and justly so." He replied that he would take it back, sell it and give me the proceeds. He got £14,000 for it, gave the sum to me, and I gave it to the Hebrew University for the purchase of a Henry Moore.'

But, whatever you have, it must be some kind of reassurance to you? 'I have never regarded my possessions as a reassurance. On the contrary, I always believed that as long as I retained my health – a substantial enough condition – and the capacity to speak, I would have enough to live on, and that has been the case.'

Of course, money, like religion, said I, is something of a taboo among the English. 'In the middle classes, certainly, you do not talk about money. It puts certain people in an embarrassment. Moreover, anything that savours of boasting is generally held in disfavour by the middle classes.

The upper classes are much less embarrassed about talking of their wealth. And if the poor talk about money, they are talking of their own failure.'

Is it a failure to be poor? 'It is a failure to be in a position where you have to beg,' G. replied. 'In itself, however, it need be no reflection upon the individual. You,' he added, 'are an example of the virtuous and deserving poor.' This took me aback. I regard that, I said to G., as a backhanded compliment. 'It is intended to be a genuine compliment,' he rejoined.

I returned to the inhibition of the British on the subject of money, asking him whether such inhibition was emotionally related to the inhibition which stopped friendship. 'No, it is a matter of good taste,' G. replied. 'It is a subject in which you can come upon a minefield. You might, for instance, find yourself talking about money to a man who had become bankrupt the day before.'

Do you think the Jews and the English have different attitudes to money? 'They don't,' said G. 'The Jewish attitude to money is largely conditioned by the Jewish attitude to life. The Jews,' he declared – as he had declared before – 'do not regard themselves as secure or settled anywhere.' But is there, in your judgment, no particular Jewish propensity to avarice or dishonesty? I asked. 'Their propensity is rather on the other side,' he replied. 'Most people would rather trust a Jewish than a Christian banker.' I remarked that Heine once said that the Jews had invented both Christianity and Bills of Exchange, and had gained more benefit from the latter than the former. 'It is perfectly true,' said G.; 'I would endorse that.' Why do you endorse it? I asked. 'Because the Jews derive benefit largely from material things and not from spiritual things. Spirituality is a rare quality among the Jews since their religion is divorced from it. Apart from a few fanatics in

72

America, no one believes in the Jewish religion with the intensity of a Catholic monk's faith in Christianity.'

Are you saying that Judaism is a materialistic religion? 'The tenets of Judaism are obscure,' G. declared; 'very few Jews could tell you what was the basis of their faith.' ('When they can tell you, they become bores,' he mischievously added.) But are rich Jews *sui generis*, or are they like other rich people? 'No, they are not like other rich people, since their attitudes are shot through with uncertainty about their own permanence, about where they might one day be.' Nevertheless, the 'rich Jew' is often seen as the archetype of the rich man as such. 'You are citing something which derives from the viewpoint of our adversaries. Moreover, the principal affront which the Jew offers the Englishman does not lie in wealth, when he has it, but in his pretence of himself being English.'

Is the rich Jew more prone to this pretence than the poor one? 'The former is more prone to it because he can afford to dress himself up in the trappings of the Englishman. He can go to the opera in expensive seats, he can go to the races, he can go to the Henley regatta; there is almost nowhere which excludes Jews as an act of policy.'

I changed the subject to ask G. whether, given all he had said on the subject of money, his 'heart bled more for rich or poor'. 'My heart does not bleed for many people,' he replied. 'But I have more sympathy with the poor, since they have less means by which to rectify what goes wrong in their lives. If you are poor, and your wife needs a liver transplant, you have no choice but to get a divorce and a new wife,' G. jestingly declared.

It is also said that wealth has its drawbacks, I remarked. 'This is a sentimental notion,' G. replied. 'People like to think that what is unavailable to them "has its drawbacks". For some, it is comforting to think that, if you

73

have money, you have solved life's problems. You have not. If anything, you have increased them.' But that is to concede the argument that money brings its own problems, said I. 'Money does bring its own problems, including the fear of losing it. You can become obsessional. When one of the Three Musketeers came to London, having borrowed money from a servant, he rescued Charles the Second and was rewarded for his services with a large sum in gold. Having had a chest made, he went to a locksmith who provided him with a device which would fire a shot if anyone tampered with the chest – his life had changed from the moment of his reward.'

You said that you can become obsessional over fears of losing money. How do you know? Is this your experience? '*One* becomes obsessional,' said G. 'I am too balanced to be obsessional about money, even if I may be unbalanced in other ways. Indeed, I myself observe rich men making absolutely trivial economies. I had a legal partner, enormously rich, to whom the notion of spending any money was a horror. There was no economy to which he would not descend. For instance, I could not help noticing that the office toilet paper was of very various quality. This was because he used to remove it from other offices which he visited and put it in ours. In this sense his conduct was pathological.'

It seems that special virtues are required for a man to be, or to remain, rich. 'You cannot generalise. You can become rich by hard work, or by winning the football pools. There are so many ways to become rich, and not all the ways of gaining wealth can be confined within the moral code – you can become rich by trafficking in drugs.' But does wealth acquired by thrift and hard work have some virtue attached to it in your eyes? 'It depends. The same "thrift and hard work" may be allied in the real world to cunning, ruthlessness, all sorts of things. In such circumstances you cannot attribute the wealth to a moral cause. One of the easiest ways to become rich is to inherit money,' G. jocularly added; 'this calls for no moral quality except that of not antagonising your rich relatives.'

But to make money, or keep the money you've got, however you came by it, does it not help to *like* money too? 'People never pose that question to themselves,' G. said. 'They do not get up in the night saying, "I like money". It is what money can do that they like.' And what of those – there are some – who actively do not like it, or who even think it, as I suggested earlier, to be the root of all evil? 'It is exaggerated and melodramatic to say that it is the "root of all evil", even if the use to which some people put it may be the root of all evil.'

You must, however, have known people who did not like money? 'I have not, but I have known rich people who were not influenced by their wealth. They were remarkable people, and there were few of them.' I expect they were individuals rich other than by their own exertions. 'All of them inherited wealth. I have never known anyone who made money in what one might call the "business jungle" who was not changed by it.'

There is a difference in attitude to money, then, between those who have inherited it and those who have made it themselves? 'The latter are more often loath to give it away.' Why do you think that should be? 'Because it is often their only achievement in life. If they give it away, it means – in a sense – that they don't respect what they have achieved. This must be a painful emotion,' G. murmured.

Would you say that very great wealth acquired in today's world must be ill-gotten, or gained without scruple? 'It is unscrupulous to acquire it at all,' G. replied. 'But you can acquire it without descending to crime or resorting

75

to immoral means. A manufacturer of a life-saving medicine has a duty not to set the price too high. If he ignores his duty he can doubtless become a rich man, but he has a moral obligation to lower the charge. Similarly, Mrs Thatcher's decision to act, for a very large salary, as adviser to a cigarette company is plainly almost obscene.' By some accounts, it was a decision driven by greed. 'I think she is greedy. She venerates capitalism, in the sense that she thinks it a virtue *per se* to create wealth in any way as long as it is legal. I do not even think that she makes that qualification, but let us give her the benefit of the doubt.'

But why single her out, when 'making money' runs away with the money-maker so often? What about a Maxwell or a Murdoch? 'Maxwell and Murdoch cannot be put together in that way. The first was a notorious criminal, the second is a hardworking person dedicated to running newspapers.' Maybe, but making money, and more money, is the ulterior purpose of such activity, said I. 'The latter obviously has a faculty for acquiring money, but not in total disregard of moral considerations. The former was a villain.'

Nevertheless, the more money they have, the more money such money-makers seem to want. 'One cannot generalise. Some people, once set on the money-making road, cannot get off it. But such cases are less common than are the cases of those who have made their money and are happy to retain it.' Is money-making a 'creative' act, in your judgment? 'In a way it is a creative act,' G. replied. For the otherwise uncreative? 'The implication of your question points to a number of assertions that are more likely to be false than true,' said G. Such as? 'Such as that "virtue is its own reward", a highly arguable proposition. There are many others like it. It illustrates only that there are widespread misconceptions about the making of money and its social implications.'

So you do not think that making money serves in the main as a solace for the otherwise uncreative, who might have preferred to be artists or writers? 'No. In the main, successful artists also like to make money. For them, too, that is the index of success.' That does not go to my point, I said. 'If a man is preoccupied 24 hours a day with making money, keeping it, or increasing it, he cannot have time for anything else.' That still does not meet my point that money might serve certain people, perhaps many people, as a compensation for what they would rather have or do. 'That argues too perceptive a view of themselves on the part of such individuals,' said G.

You don't think, said I, that many of the wealthy might prefer to be poor-but-talented painters or musicians? 'No generalisation is possible. Moreover, the rich are seldom interested in "culture". This is particularly noticeable in the case of rich Jews. Very few of them even have an interest in Jewish education.' Nevertheless, they can and do acquire the trappings of a cultured existence, I said. 'In the sense that someone has told them that it is good taste to hang an Impressionist on the wall, they will buy one. But, in the main, they are uneducated.' This would only be surprising if to become wealthy required education, said I. 'Education is irrelevant to the acquisition of wealth,' said G.

Do you think it is actually a handicap to money-making? 'Not so much a handicap. The basic way in which Robert Maxwell acquired his wealth was by an educated method. He made available some of the knowledge of this country, including its scientific knowledge, to others. In a way this was admirable. The side-roads he travelled were not admirable at all.' But didn't his fall also reveal how hard it is to remain honest while pursuing riches? 'It is hard to remain honest, full stop,' G. replied. 'The average person is not in support of dishonesty,' he continued. 'But it is difficult for him to resist all the temptations that come his way. A man who goes to church, synagogue or mosque will not hesitate to defraud the Inland Revenue, because he sees that as a different kind of morality.'

Does it follow that one of the temptations of wealth is the possibility it provides of ignoring everyday morality? I asked. 'You have to be a very strong character,' G. answered, 'not to succumb to the temptations of wealth, the temptations of luxury, or the joys of widespread travel, and travelling well and in comfort. I do not do a great deal of travelling,' G. added, 'but perhaps I would be morally better without such temptations.'

But what about the serious temptations of wealth, the temptation to purchase favours, services and honours, and even to purchase other people?

'You have to arrive at a sensible conception of how to use the money you have. If an individual sees people selling honours on all sides, for instance, he could readily succumb to saying, "I'd like one, too, why not?" Money is also useful in enlisting the help and support of great numbers of people who are, it could be said, on the market to be bribed or paid.' One could not object to some of it, I said. 'It makes the world go round. It is the staple of business transactions. There is very little difference in morality between the activities of a grocer's shop in Stamford Hill and Selfridge's. Both are trying to sell something at more than it is worth so that the difference can sustain the interests of the vendor.'

Where do you draw the line between the moral and the immoral use of money? 'It becomes reprehensible when it takes on an anti-social aspect, as when a single individual buys all the coffee in the world and corners the market. It is not reprehensible to keep a grocery shop and sell coffee to the community for a fair price. Money is misused when its employment is in conflict with good conduct, or inconsistent with good intentions.' Can you give other examples? 'To put on a pornographic play in the West End of London to the detriment of other plays, to buy a football club so as to ensure that its management no longer proceeds on democratic principles, totally to appropriate the services of a doctor when those services are needed by others . . .' What is the common quality of such abuses? 'They are done in conscious disregard of morality,' G. answered.

Nevertheless, I said, you cannot legislate against most of them. 'You cannot legislate for virtue, that is true,' said G. In which case, your principles rely merely upon the hope of good sense in the possessors of the resources. 'They depend on the operation of social sanctions to penalise the misuse of their powers,' said G. Yes, but such social sanctions – against greed, for example – have never been less in evidence than now. 'That does not affect the validity of the social sanctions themselves, where they exist.'

Have you yourself ever lent or borrowed money?' I asked G. 'It was Polonius in *Hamlet* who said "Neither a borrower nor a lender be". It is certainly a good principle, in theory, not to borrow money, but it is a bad principle never to lend it.' Have you? 'I have certainly lent it. I have also had people give me money for particular purposes. But I have not borrowed money consciously.' Had you been in need, would you have borrowed? 'That is impossible to say. But if I knew that my flat had to be sold up tomorrow, I would hopefully find someone to lend me what I required.'

You don't see any moral objection to borrowing and lending? 'If a person in need borrows money, I cannot see any objection to it. In fact, he has to do it. But if he were to come to you and say, "I'll commit suicide in the morning if you don't lend me what I need", one has a moral duty to let him commit suicide,' G. declared sardonically. Have you had the experience? 'A number of people I have known have threatened suicide, but not for lack of money. In every case, they were wealthy people wanting to get clear of this awful world. Maxwell was a good example of it, a man who was in despair at the situation in which he found himself. But I have not known many suicides of people who were close to me. Three or four attempts were made which might have been exhibitionist. Another three or four succeeded, but no more than that.' That was surely enough, I said. 'They were all associated with some kind of mental weakness,' said G. briefly.

Do many people throw themselves on your mercy *in extremis*? 'People have come to me contemplating suicide. In one or two cases I was unable to avert it. A certain individual, who had been a total failure in publishing, came to tea one Sunday saying that he could not go on. I tried to soothe him, but he killed himself that night.' Did you feel guilty? 'I did not feel guilty. I felt that I had failed, and that I should have been able to talk him out of it.'

Perhaps, I said, not even money and success would have made a difference. Money, after all, can't buy you love. 'In the abstract, that is probably true,' said G., with some hesitation. Or can it? 'What it can buy you is the belief that you can buy love,' he answered. 'Until you get to the next world, it is not possible to say whether such a belief was true or not.' Nevertheless, said I, there are men who are convinced that it is not easy to sustain the love of at least some women without money. 'But there is certainly a form of affection which can exist devoid of any financial considerations,' said G. 'There is also an idyllic period – perhaps as long as a day – in which two young people can believe in a love which has no material requirements.'

Don't you think it is hard to sustain some other types of social relationship without money? The relationships you have sustained, for example? 'If you belong to any class of society which functions within perceptible boundaries, you need money to remain within them,' G. now said. The relationships established within these 'boundaries' would soon founder without money? 'Probably,' G. answered. While those on the outside of these 'boundaries', looking in, are likely to be jealous of what they see? 'The best exponent of the relative value of money and of true human qualities was George Bernard Shaw,' said G., by way of reply. 'He did not believe that, in comparing them, money was worth what it is believed to be worth.'

Nevertheless, those without money have a habit of believing it to be worth more than Shaw thinks it is worth. Don't you think that the less rich are often attracted to the more rich in the hope of benefiting from them, or at least of getting crumbs from their table? 'It is rare for people to toady to others from the prospect of money being given to them,' G. answered. But I imagine that the rich must be suspicious of some of those who cluster around them? 'The rich are certainly more suspicious of the poor than the poor are of the rich,' said G.

Do you also think the social gap between the rich and the poor is widening? 'With the increase in popular entertainment it is getting narrower, not wider. The rich and the poor go to the same opera – if in different seats – attend the same football match, and watch the same television programmes. There is a great degree of *sameness*, which cannot be greatly modified by having money.' Is the extent of this 'sameness' increasing? 'It is rather the nature of class which has changed. But it is difficult for a Jew to assess such change.' Why? 'Because the Jews can belong to any class to which they elect to belong,' G. replied. (That the Jews might not be able to make true judgments about class was a proposition from which the Jewish Marx would have dissented.)

Is money-obsession akin to other forms of obsession, do you think? 'It may be identical with the collector's urge,' G. answered. 'But there are many individuals who collect things without regard to their value. Those are the true collectors,' he added. How, I asked G., would you explain my doctor-father's daily entry in his diary – or 'ledger', as he often called it – of every smallest detail of his expenditure? Was that not obsession? 'No. He was a man of immensely meticulous habits in general. One of these habits was associated with the management of his financial position. He was merely wise enough never to enter into a transaction beyond his means.' But for a busy physician to record the spending of a few pence on sweets? 'He was obviously a person who had not grown up with money. He was not indifferent to it. But in his preoccupation with it there was nothing vicious. It did not detract from his moral qualities. On the contrary, it added to them.'

Did you keep such meticulous oversight over your financial affairs? 'I never kept it at all,' G. replied, laughing. But you must have exerted some control over your financial position. 'I roughly examined the situation from time to time with one eye on bankruptcy,' said G. jovially. 'Once I was satisfied that that was not my condition, I carried on as normal. I was never extravagant, but there was no sign of meanness or special care in my spending. I could not lead a life in which I counted the pennies.' When does my father's kind of meticulousness become parsimony? 'I do not think that thrift is necessarily the same as parsimony,' G. replied. 'Not that counting pennies is necessarily thrift,' he added. 'It obviously starts in extreme youth. In my family's household there was little money, but no one worried about it. My mother was a marvellous manager who tried to give us everything we needed. She made a brave show.'

'Petty cash' is to you truly petty, then? 'That would give the impression that I was concerned about large cash instead. I was concerned with neither. I had other things to think about.'

[6]

America

G. had told me last week that he wanted to speak of
America, which he had visited 'on a number of occasions,
but never for very long'. Had his forbears from Lithuania
not stayed in England but continued on to America, as so
many Jewish migrants did, I said, he might have been an
American not an English Jew. How, I asked, would he
now regard *that* as an alternative personal fate? With
equanimity? 'That is an artificial question,' he answered.
'If I had seen America for the first time when I was in
possession of all my reasoning powers, I would not have
wanted to stay there.'

Why not? 'I do not like the vulgarity of American life,'
he answered. 'I do not like a philosophy wholly related to
the dollar, I do not like the American academic world . . .'
This was said with force. But, I interjected – he was on the
point of adding to his list – you have described yourself to
me as 'not an Englishman' but as an 'English Jew'. He
nodded agreement. In which case, I might have expected
you to claim yourself to be a 'citizen of the world', and as
able to conceive of yourself as an American as anything
else. 'To claim to be a "citizen of the world" is a silly
thing,' G. said with some heat. 'It means nothing. You

cannot be a citizen of "the world". The world is too variegated and large to give it sense.' But could you not reasonably feel, as a Jew, English or any other, that you were at home anywhere? 'No,' G. replied. 'That would show some failure of sincerity. Nobody is "at home anywhere". I would not be at home in the middle of the Sahara Desert without a water-bottle,' he continued with renewed bonhomie, 'nor in the frozen wastes of Iceland. There are many places I am not at home, but I am thoroughly at home in England.'

You are plainly not 'at home' in the United States, I said. 'I am not conscious of being "at home", or not "at home" there. The longest time I have ever stayed was a fortnight. But it was long enough to realise that I did not wish to make it my home, even though I have very many friends there who are charming, erudite and generous. The average American,' he added, 'is a Babbitt.'

Do you then have a positive antipathy to America and Americans as such? 'Not an antipathy. But I dislike their philosophy, their social ethics, their obvious preoccupation with material things. These remain in contrast with much that is taken for granted in this country.' Nevertheless, I said, there is felt to be something called an 'Anglo-American' world, which has certain political and other principles in common. Do you not feel part of it? 'I have never thought about it. But I do not regard myself as a member of any "Anglo-American world". If I am a member of anything in this respect, it is of an Anglo-European world.'

Do you not concede that there are such affinities between the citizens of Britain and America that 'Anglo-American' could have a meaning? What about American Anglophilia, for instance? 'I do not think of anyone as an Anglo-American. In America, to identify with Britain and the British way of life is merely a social position.' You mean it is a form of snobbery? 'It could be called snobbery. It is usually a question of liking, or admiring, the habits of upper-class Englishmen and wanting to emulate them.'

But surely the British and the Americans share certain substantial traditions, a belief in representative democracy, the rule of law, and so on? 'To some extent. Much of it is attributable to the mistaken belief that we speak the same language. But we are a long way from ironing out even more substantial differences.' Your remark about language must be a jest, I said. 'No,' G. replied. 'If you read an American novel it could not have been written by an Englishman, and vice-versa.'

What are these 'substantial differences'? 'Differences, first, in social assumptions and habits. In the British middle and upper classes it is quite common to have servants, for instance. For all but rich Americans, this is an exceptional situation. It derives in England from a very healthy out-look. No one, or very few, in England would regard it as ignominious, as do the Americans, to render personal service.' Even if this is true, surely you are not reducing the 'substantial differences' between the British and the Americans to this? 'It is obviously not the major differ-ence.' Is it important at all? 'It is very important.' Why? 'Because it demonstrates differences in attitude between the English and the Americans towards the rest of mankind.

'An American also has a distinct approach to amiability and friendship. He may, in many instances, be as slow as the Englishman to demonstrate them. But his reserve does not take long to wear off. If you take a taxi in New York, you are often greeted with an unreasoning hostility. "Why," the cab driver seems to say to himself, "should he travel in my cab?" But in a few moments the barrier is broken.' What about the London cabbie, and his readiness for banter and political discussion? 'Leaving aside cab-drivers,' G. said, 'the attitude of the Englishman is that he has a duty to remain aloof. The American feels he has no such duty.'

But all this, I said, could be considered trivial. What do you think of the old attitude of the British left, exemplified by Michael Foot, say, that the United States was, in some sort, a Babylon? 'That stems from a political view of America as the mecca of capitalism, where good honest European socialists should not set foot,' G. replied. You too have hinted at a recoil from the world of the almighty dollar, similar enough to the recoil of the left, said I. 'I share the prejudice which is opposed to the conservative viewpoint,' said G. 'Often the American viewpoint is conservative in ways to which I am opposed, and remote from the British temper.'

How? 'In the McCarthy period,' G. replied, 'it was clear that the Americans had not learned the civilised practices of a substantial part of mankind. At that time, horrors were committed which we could not regard as acceptable. That some of those brought under accusation by Senator McCarthy could not find lawyers to represent them ran counter to the values of English law and practice. The persecution of individuals by rumour is more prevalent in America than in England.'

As early as the 1830s, I said to G., De Tocqueville had remarked upon the American journalist's 'vulgar turn of mind' and written of how he 'habitually assails the char-acters of individuals' in order to 'track them into private life and disclose all their weaknesses and errors.' 'Just as the tabloids in Britain do now,' commented G. The American habit has spread since then, said I. 'It is not Americans, but the Murdochs and the Maxwells who have been responsible for it here,' G. now declared. 'But they have been driven to develop a business practice consistent with the competition for readers. One thing that attracts people is the abuse of their fellow-men,' G. added. Judging by De Tocqueville, however, the modern provenance of these and related press excesses is American, said I. 'Dickens denounced the American press more than a century ago for its abuse of his copyright without reward, and such practices obtained there until very late. It showed a significant difference in the American approach to the artist from that of the British,' said G.

Was it fair of De Tocqueville to imply that there was a 'vulgar turn of mind' among Americans in general? For instance, he also referred to the 'vulgar demeanour' of the members of the House of Representatives in Washington. 'No judgment is fair which relates to everybody. If some people and institutions in America, especially their legal system in public trials, display a "vulgar turn of mind" it is, however, fair to draw attention to it,' G. replied. 'It is also the fact that television in America has developed at a much greater pace than anywhere else in the world, and has offered attractions of the lowest possible level to the largest possible number of the public.'

That might, to some Americans, sound a very English type of snobbery, I said. 'I do not think I am an English snob,' G. responded. 'I may have absorbed some English values, but my criticisms are not governed by snobbishness. Indeed, there was a time when the English upper class used to regard as superior anyone American. Hence, their enthusiasm for American heiresses.' But there was often a snobbish antipathy to the 'vulgar American' too? 'There was, but it was not sufficiently deep to resist the blandishments of other people's wives,' said G., with a brief chuckle.

In any case, said I, there is some vulgarity or other, in the sense in which De Tocqueville meant it, to be found in every nation. 'You can find it in England, but not as a national characteristic,' said G. 'A football crowd could be called a "vulgar assembly", but that would not be a fair description of those who are enthusiastic about a certain game and derive social comfort from attending it.' What about the 'football hooligan' who sets out to carve up the fans of an opposing team? 'That is a question of discipline, a different matter. The average English crowd is less disciplined than the average American crowd.'

America surely has other virtues to be approved of than the greater discipline of its sports fans? 'They have displayed an astonishing generosity in their foreign policy. Without the Marshall Plan we would have been in a terrible mess in Europe. On two occasions, they joined Britain and her European allies in world wars which might easily have been lost if they had not been there. Their public image for such kind of actions is among the best in the world. It has been nullified to some extent since the Second War by the fact that purely political considerations have played so large a part in influencing American actions, but the image has not lost value.'

But what about the dynamism of American life? Does that too not have its value? 'The tempo of life, particularly in New York, is faster and more exhausting than in England,' G. replied. Is it merely exhausting? 'No,' said G., 'but at the end of seven or ten days there, you are more than happy to go home.' Would you not say that it offered exhilaration as well as exhaustion? 'American hospitality is exhausting,' G. persisted. 'If you have a great number of acquaintances, the knowledge that you have arrived is a trumpet-blast to entertainment. They would regard it as disobliging not to entertain you.' Is that not a virtue by your own criteria of friendship? 'A week in New York is a week of socialising. That is a different matter.'

I thought you enjoyed it, said I. 'Not entirely. But it is a happy contrast with a week in London, where if you were to arrive as a single stranger you would spend your seven days never speaking to anyone except bus conductors.' How do you think your American friends perceive you? I asked. As an English eccentric? 'Some, for whom I feel deep affection, regard me as a particularly amiable example of British culture,' G. replied. You don't disabuse them? I ventured. 'I carry on as before,' said G..

But you are seen in America as the embodiment of what, exactly? 'I am seen,' G. answered wryly, 'as something of particular interest, because they do not know where else to look for it. When I arrive, they welcome what they are expecting, which is a totally independent viewpoint, a willingness to say anything about anybody – subject to considerations of decency – a man whom they like to introduce into their world. It is all very flattering. I am sure there are contrary sentiments to these which I have not encountered,' G. added.

I take it that in America you are perceived to be more an Englishman than a Jew? 'Anti-semitism is more rampant in America than in this country,' he answered. 'It is a nation split into tiny communities with narrow outlook and limited culture, where a disease like anti-semitism can prosper, can burgeon. I have never encountered it personally in America, but I know that it is there and that I would not have to go far to meet it head-on. But it is not a sensible thing to do. If I do meet it, however, as in my reaction to the Duchess of York [when G. refused to continue acting as her legal adviser, after she had attended an American country club which barred Jews from its membership], I am not prepared to compromise with it.'

Do you not admire American business energy? 'I have not been involved with it for many years, and never sufficiently involved to take an approving or disapproving view. But the effect of their social philosophy on so many people is a different matter. It is genuinely believed in America, and not as a joke, that in everyone's knapsack – many do not even have a knapsack – there is a field-marshal's baton. But it is a merciless notion that if you have not been successful it is your own silly fault. Its consequence is that no one is satisfied with his lot. Every taxi-driver yearns to be a lawyer or a business tycoon, and believes that with effort and good fortune he can be. The American philosophy of life justifies that faith.'

Is that a bad thing? I asked. 'It is not a good thing or a bad thing,' G. answered. 'If it brings comfort to the unsuccessful, who can go on hoping for ever, it is a good thing. It keeps alive the sort of hope that the American lift-boy has when he says that he is studying at night-school in order to go to university. Here, people submit much more readily to the accidents of their birth. It makes more conspicuous in Britain those who have shaken off their chains. But the American philosophy can be cruel in its effects, when the individual discovers that in his knapsack there is no field-marshal's baton.'

What kind of field-marshal is the average American lawyer? I inquired. 'There is a wider variety of choice and disposition in the American than in the British legal system,' said G., by way of answer. 'American law is less conventional and less tied by tradition than the British and has achieved a high level of justice. Many would regard the American Supreme Court as the outstanding court in the world in respect to its judges' learning and integrity, even if there have been more instances to arouse doubt about it than in the case of the higher courts in England.'

Do you share the approving view on the part of the 'many' about the US Supreme Court? 'Yes, I do. But the extent to which prejudice can determine court judgments in the United States is greater than in England. Take the case of Alger Hiss. It is clear to me that what he was convicted of was being a member of the Communist Party.' There was always more paranoia about communism in America than in Britain, I said. 'That is because their society is more firmly based on possessions than any other. Communism was a terrible threat to possession and wealth, and a large part of American political thinking is devoted to the protection of wealth.'

Are you implying that the Americans stand in need of a greater leaven of European or even English culture and sophistication, including political sophistication? 'Not at all. They have an ample complement of their own cultural and educational institutions. There are more universities – and more average universities – in America than anywhere in the world, largely owing to the generosity of their alumni. But it is also true that their educational standards at every level are lower than ours, even if it is difficult to find anything of much lower standard than our own elementary education, in which children can leave primary schools unable to read or write.' Statistics suggest that there are now millions, even tens of millions, of illiterate and semi-literate people in the United States. 'It is the blackboard jungle. Lacking is discipline. Indiscipline in many American schools, so I am told, is terrifying.'

Do you see America in general as a Promethean force and 'Americanisation' as a danger to the culture of others? 'The miscellany of American life,' G. answered cautiously, 'emerges as more satisfactory than one might have cause to think. In American small towns, for all their narrowness, there is a camaraderie and concern for the community. In many British towns people never speak to one another.' Do you mean that American civic virtues are their saving grace? 'I am saying that there is a stronger sense of community in America than in Britain. No one in Britain struts about declaring "I am a citizen of Eastbourne", or, on a higher level, of Bournemouth,' G. said with a laugh. 'People here are embarrassed about making declarations of fidelity to their country and their race. In America they are not in the least embarrassed about it.'

Why are they more ready to make such declarations in America? 'One explanation is that so many Americans are immigrants, anxious to sink roots in the country and to advertise the fact that they have done so. No one in England is bursting with pride that they were born in Woking.' How do you know? 'It is based on secondary evidence. I am prepared to assert it without knowing it directly. ('I don't know much of what I am saying directly,' G. added merrily.) In many cases in this country, civic pride attaches to an institution like the local football club, but not to the town itself.'

Is the relative absence of civic pride a serious defect? 'We are the poorer in this country for lacking it. We send teams abroad with thousands of hooligans to support them. It is not an admirable trait. Instead of bringing out the best in people, and in the absence of true civic pride, pride of a territorial or national nature brings out the worst. In Britain, it sends people abroad, armed with razor blades and bludgeons, whose sole object is the murdering and maiming of their fellow men.' This was said with mirth.

But the Americans, with their murder rates, can teach us a thing or two about violence. 'Of course they can,' G. replied. 'That is because America is a larger country, with a population of many different origins. They have their

93

mafias . . .' And go to sleep in New York, I interjected, to the sound of gunfire. '. . . They even seem to relish the disorder. Ed McBain writes entirely about the underworld of New York; reading him you get the impression that this underworld is by no means disapproved of morally by the rest of the community. Certain film stars, such as James Cagney, depended on an adulation of violence.'

You are not an admirer of 'Hollywood culture'? 'No, not at all. However, it has not done as much damage as pedants and prigs suggest. It has provided interest for the lesser intellects of the world. Moreover, usually, the morality of Hollywood films is reasonably good, except in relation to violence.' That is a large exception, I said. 'But it is a violence which does not necessarily express any approval of it on the part of the film-makers. The approval is in the people who swarm to see violent films. The makers of such films merely pander to the tastes of the public.'

That is itself a vicious circle. 'Yes, but the suggestion that bad behaviour is induced by seeing films, or books, is to a large extent mythical. Original sin is in everyone, and can be brought out in original ways. The reading of a book can often be a valid excuse for committing a savage murder. The terror that the Mary Whitehouses of this world feel is based on an excessive belief in the example that might be set by scenes of sex or violence which they do not like. Time and time again, scientific investigation shows that the extent to which bad behaviour can be influenced by their criteria is small.'

Have you gained any benefit and pleasure from American culture? 'A considerable amount from American drama,' G. replied. 'Today, it is the most distinguished drama in the world. One leaves the theatre uplifted after seeing a play by Tennessee Williams or Arthur Miller. But jazz means nothing to me.' I expect that you would not go out of your way to listen to Frank Sinatra. 'I would go out of my way to avoid listening to Frank Sinatra,' G. chuckled. What about pop music? 'I have no ear for pop music, American or any other. More truthfully, I have an ear which is resistant to it. One of the mysteries of modern-day culture is how loutish youths with voices like corn-crakes can attain popular eminence. But it goes on happening,' he added with good humour.

Why do you call it a mystery? I asked. 'It is not really a mystery,' G. replied. 'The solution to the question of how the audience for pop music is recruited is quite simple. We have devised a system of omitting to educate 99 per-cent of the population. This is a deliberate choice. It is not surprising that the 99 per-cent do not have elevated tastes when they have not been introduced to the great literature of the world, for example. In Britain, less than one in 10 people visits the theatre. A large number would not know how to visit a theatre and buy a seat, or what to do with their coats when they arrived. This situation can only be rectified by providing more money for the instructors in the arts. But the extent to which the governing classes in this country loathe the arts is a fact that has to be recognised by those who are trying to rectify the situation.'

Has the vulgarisation of our taste, if such it is, come from across the Atlantic? 'It cannot be attributed to that cause. It is indigenous.' Nevertheless, the 'Disneyland' syndrome has a long reach, as the French know, I said. Doesn't 'Americanisation' hold any terrors for you? 'The American population is derived from a variety of colourful races, largely arriving in the United States in their teens, uneducated. Many, despite the educational opportunities, never obtained, and continue not to obtain in America, the kind of education which a civilised taste requires. You must expect from it social consequences which are disobliging,' said G..

And I take it, from what you have already said, that English educational reforms look no more encouraging to you? 'Disrespect for education has been manifested in Britain by governments of both colours. In particular, I remain to be impressed by the argument that parents should play a vital part in controlling their children's education. Aneurin Bevan once remarked that the best fate a child can have is to be removed from its parents at birth.'

Nevertheless, I said, both societies, American and British, are now struggling in various ways to raise their educational standards. 'The American system of education, despite its defects, has some advantages over ours. A large percentage of children get as far as high school, and the proportion of college entrants is much higher in America, even if it is largely because standards are much lower.'

Are such phenomena – like the American recoil from rendering personal service to which you referred earlier – to be placed among the virtues or the vices of American democracy? I asked G. 'Any attempt to improve generally the educational level of mankind could be described as a vice of democracy or as a virtue of democracy,' G. carefully replied. Where do you stand? 'I come down somewhere in the middle.' I observed that De Tocqueville, more than a century and a half ago, had declared that although there was a great deal of talent in the American people, American leaders tended to be men of little distinction; he thought it a product of democratic excess that the 'lower orders', as he put it, found 'superiority' in their leaders to be 'irksome'. Hence, De Tocqueville believed the most distinguished citizens in America could not advance in the political system without 'degrading themselves'.

'Disinclination for political life is essentially the same in many countries,' G. commented. 'You expose yourself to the sort of attention which the sensible man avoids. Political office could only be sought by an ambitious man unselective in the company he keeps.'

And in the American case, the people can then end up with a 'mountebank' like Reagan, for example, who 'knows the secrets of stimulating its tastes', to use De Tocqueville's words? 'That is an individual opinion,' said G.. 'But the nature of a nation's political life must have a large part to play in the nature and quality of its political leaders. An uneducated, or only sparsely educated, electorate will have the misfortune to be receptive to every prejudice which is about. If you study political leaders' pronouncements today, one of their salient qualities is often an uninformed prejudice, a prejudice which also meets popular requirements.'

As in Reagan's case? 'You have to look at the whole structure of public life. Its demands would discourage most decent people. The fact that Reagan had never read a book, lacked diversity of culture, and had no knowledge of any substantial kind was not regarded with disapproval by the generality of the population. He was seen by the Americans as "one of us". The miracle is that individuals of quality have ever prevailed in American and British political life. Roosevelt and Attlee were among them.' Not Churchill? 'He does not fit into any category.' He was not, to you, a man of virtue? 'Not of virtue, but of outstanding achievements.'

Is the dearth of fitting leaders really due to the fact that 'superiority' is found 'irksome' by others? 'There is truth in that. As Nye Bevan once said, the worst thing that can happen to a politician is that he should be regarded as clever.' Surely you would bemoan that? 'My bemoaning it would make no difference,' G. replied with equanimity. But it was the kind of attitude which disqualified an Adlai Stevenson and promoted a Reagan, said I. 'Reagan,' G. responded mordantly, 'was a popular film star. Adlai Stevenson had a suspect reputation for being cultivated, clever and witty. These were characteristics regarded as unacceptable by the majority.'

Do you not lament that kind of thing? 'If I went about lamenting what is wrong with our societies, I would be sitting cross-legged weeping most of the day. I have endeavoured, in my own scheme of life, to rectify the situation whenever I could.' Have you succeeded? 'By a millimetre.'

7

On Europeans – and Germany

The last time we talked, I said, you declared yourself unsympathetic to the idea that there was an 'Anglo-American' culture and rejected the proposition that you might consider yourself a part of it. Instead, you were, you said, an Anglo-European if you were anything. What does that mean? And is not the idea of Europe the utopia of our times? 'At the moment, interest in Europe in this country is at its height,' G. replied. 'Which is not to say,' he added, 'that that is very high. This is because, in the main, England has benefited from being an island, even if in some particular, it has also suffered.'

But is the idea of 'Europe', as it is presented to us in arguments about the benefits of belonging to the European Community, merely a chimera? I repeated. 'It is not a chimera for some people,' G. (characteristically) replied. 'But for the general population the concept of "Europe" has neither meaning nor importance.' Is that a just assessment on their part? 'It is a just assessment,' answered G. briefly. The concept of 'Europe' may have no meaning for many, said I, but 'Europe' as a travel destination, say, has real significance for large numbers of people?

'It is still true that the majority of the citizens of the

country have never visited "Europe".' Some eighteen million Britons go abroad each year, I interjected. 'That is certainly a large minority,' G. said. 'But it is still a minority. The majority have no personal experience of Europe even as tourists, let alone as partisans of the "European idea".' Despite G.'s insistence that a majority of the British had neither interest in, nor knowledge of, 'Europe', I felt the need to resist what he was saying.

'Let us call in Molly' [his daily help], G. unexpectedly proposed, telling me to go to the kitchen to summon her, which I did. ('Good God!' I heard her declare at the summons.) A woman in her early fifties, she entered and stood bashfully by the dining table, like a serving-maid in an eighteenth-century novel, brought before the master of the household to be interrogated. 'Have you ever been to Europe?' G. demanded of her, surely knowing beforehand what her answer would be. 'Never, sir,' she replied. 'I have never been to London either,' she added for good measure, beaming. But I'm sure that you have not got many friends who have not been to London, said I. 'No,' she admitted, 'I haven't.' 'Nevertheless,' said G. genially, dismissing my exchange, 'you see that Molly has never been to Europe. Do you have any desire to go to Europe?' he asked her. 'No, sir,' she replied. 'Thank you,' declared G., with the air of triumph of a prosecuting counsel who has worsted an opponent.

This was less than convincing evidence in itself of a national unconcern for 'Europe', but G. proceeded as if it was the most persuasive of proofs. 'My assertion that a great number of people know nothing of Europe,' G. continued, as she left the room, 'can be extended to the assertion that a large number of people in the provinces have never been to London. They have never been to London because it holds no interest for them, just as they have never been to 'Europe' because it holds no interest for them either.'

If this is so (which I did not concede), on what does the supposed British aspiration to be 'part of Europe' then rest? I asked. 'This idea of "Europe" as a location to which we should be closer is basically an idea found among a small number of people who are educated. Thus, if you can speak a European language well, you will probably want to go to the country in which it is spoken. If, however, you cannot speak a word of any such language – can barely speak English either – you will not be avid for European travel.'

What you are saying is that the 'idea of Europe' is an idea confined to a few intellectuals? 'The interest in, and even enthusiasm for, "Europe" is largely one that has been manufactured by the serious newspapers and certain magazines like the *Spectator* or the *New Statesman*, which are read by the educated. They proceed on the basis that everyone is either "pro-European" or "anti-European". But the great majority of people have no attitude to "Europe", because they have no interest in it at all. Instead, they thank the Almighty for having provided a Channel between England and the "Continent", and for sparing them the need to debate whether they are or are not "European".'

So the idea of Europe, in your judgment, is little more than an intellectual artifice? 'It is part of the stock-in-trade of a small minority of people, largely politicians. It gives them something to talk about, when otherwise they would be largely speechless. One can see how a relatively intelligent person, like the Prime Minister, adopted it as a theme, while seeking simultaneously not to outrage his supporters. Yet he is not a natural "European". I would be interested to know how often he had visited the countries of Europe before he became prime minister. I would also be most surprised if he spoke any other tongue than his own,' G. added.

This in itself is not proof, said I, that the issue of 'Europe' engages as few people as you maintain. 'The issue of "Europe" is of real, vital interest to a very small number of people,' G. insisted. A holiday on the Costa Brava or attendance at a European football fixture has left no mark, then, on the ordinary British consciousness? 'An over-whelming number of British people have never been to Europe. Investigation would reveal it. There may be journalistic interest in the Costa Brava, not least as a safe refuge for a number of outstanding British criminals, but I am convinced that the whole matter of "Europe" is of interest to relatively few.'

In which case, the 'European community' cannot be a community at all? 'It cannot be a "community" because there is too large an impulse in too many people in the countries of Europe to resist belonging to a "community".' But don't the countries of Europe constitute a community willy-nilly? 'Only by accident of juxtaposition,' G. replied. You are then sceptical about the whole business of 'Europe'. 'I am sceptical that a great number of people have a loyalty to Europe, when that loyalty could only be in conflict with their patriotisms in relation to their respective countries.'

Could it then be said that the idea of 'Europe', of 'getting closer' to 'Europe', and all the rest of it is an illusory and even dangerous panacea for British ills? 'Not dangerous,' G. replied. 'But you would have had to be of outstanding naïveté to have believed that after "going into Europe" – whatever that may mean – all would be well. You would have had to be of similar naïveté to have believed that all would be ill. A balanced judgment about this is very much a matter of education. Educated people on the whole have visited, and may in some instances know well and like, one or other of the European countries, France or Italy for example. Among them, such a degree of naïveté is, in general, less common.'

Were we at fault in going into Europe? 'No. As a moral undertaking, and even as a commercial undertaking, it was a sensible thing to do. The Common Market achieved by artificial means – by treaties, removal of barriers and so forth – what the Americans had naturally. It provides a wider market. But so many extraneous issues have been confused with it, such as the question of "sovereignty".' Surely, the issue is important? 'If you asked the majority of people if they set much store by "sovereignty",' G. replied quickly, 'they would not know what you meant.' Are you also saying that the 'sovereignty of parliament' is of no real significance, or that we have nothing to lose to Brussels? 'We would be losing something hallowed by the years,' said G. 'But if you set in motion an inquiry to find out if most Englishmen value their "sovereignty", you would first have to explain to them what it was.'

They would surely care about losing the right to govern their own country, said I. 'They do not govern their own country,' G. replied. 'They have the right to evict a government every four or five years, which is a different matter. What that government has done in those four or five years they might be advised to leave unexamined if they wished to continue to believe in their "sovereignty",' G. added. But that is very different from the suggestion that the debate over European political union, say, is a lather about nothing, or nothing very much? 'It is of great national significance that we have good relations with our neighbours,' G. replied. 'In the past, bad relations with them have produced appalling wars.'

Nevertheless, said I, you seem to be discounting the reasons for the ardour of some in Britain for closer European ties. Why should Edward Heath, for example, have pushed the 'European ideal' as if his life depended on it? Or was he one of the small minority of intellectuals enamoured of the 'idea of Europe' as such? 'Edward Heath was not an intellectual,' G. answered with a chuckle, 'he was a clever man. "The word intellectual needs avoiding at all times.) He saw a romantic prospect of borders being disposed of and such like, and, in a broad sense, of people living in a freer world. But you only have to be a Yugoslav refugee trying to get into this country to realise how un-Europeanised we are.'

Are the English not European in any event, whatever they may think of Brussels bureaucrats and the rest? 'The Channel did things for us of great value, as well as of a certain inconvenience. It rendered it impossible for us to say we are "part of Europe" . . .' G. began. You surely don't mean, I interrupted, that there is no sense in which the British can call themselves Europeans? 'In a geographical sense we are Europeans in the same sense that Ghanaians can describe themselves as Africans,' said G. Are you actually claiming that there are no values the British share with 'Europeans' or that there is no such thing as European civilisation? 'There is a European civilisation in the sense that the countries of Europe would lay claim to share certain values,' said G., 'however ill-defined.'

Do these values not exist and have any substance? 'As I see it,' G. replied, 'the term "European" might be said at most to signify a degree of civilisation in excess of the norm, such as in showing good behaviour towards other people. There are also some things which could be said to be un-European. To boil an individual in oil could be considered wholly un-European,' G. chuckled, 'even if somewhere in Europe such a fate is no doubt being prepared for someone.'

To be a 'European' country is no token, in your judgment, of a standard of general civility? 'To suggest that it is,' G. replied briskly, 'is an excellent illustration of building houses without bricks.' In what sense? 'There is no strong supporting evidence to show that any country in Europe conforms sufficiently to an idea of civility in its philosophy, life-styles, morality, legal practices or constitutional arrangements for such a claim to be made.' It is not a token of 'culture' either, in your estimation? 'I would not judge people by their culture. I might judge them by their lack of culture, or more important, their opposition to culture.'

Do you hear any racist resonance in the term 'European', as some blacks might? 'It has the connotation only that it is better to be civilised in Europe than barbaric in Africa.' You are not saying that all Africans are barbarians? 'No, but a good many are.' So what is Europe? 'The conception of Europe is a piece of geography, not an ethical conception,' G. roundly declared. 'Does Turkey meet the criteria of "civility"?' G. asked rhetorically. Turkey is not in the European community, I said. 'Does Greece?' G. asked instead.

But surely you regard yourself as in some sense a European? 'I might regard myself as "European" in the sense of having a larger knowledge of the European arts, its music, its painting, its drama, than most people. This does not mean that my knowledge is vast,' G. added. 'But if I am able to say that I prefer Beethoven to Gilbert and Sullivan, the preference gives rise to a rather thin claim to be a European.' Although you seem to wish to avoid the term, you must have some sense of the meaning of European, if only because you regard the Turks, for example, as 'beyond the pale'? 'No,' said G. flatly. 'I cannot feel any special affinity to the French either. The Turks have a more reputable record than the French in their treatment of the Jews. There was never a Dreyfus case in Turkey.' Do you know that? 'It is an observation based on a massive ignorance of Turkish history,' G. replied with a laugh.

Does your feeling of 'affinity' with a nation then depend on its treatment of the Jews? 'It is bound to be a very significant aspect of it,' said G. 'If I believed that a particular people was, for example, cruel to small boys, that would not weigh with me as much as its treatment of the Jews. It is not the only criterion for a sense of affinity. But one of the most important is whether you feel at home in the presence of particular people. I do not feel at home with the French. The basic reason for that is their attitude to the Jews. The Dreyfus case was not a solitary aberration. There are still people in France who consider Dreyfus to have been a traitor.'

I gather from all this, said I, that any 'falling apart' of Europe would, logically, not have much significance. 'Not when the term "falling apart", used in such a context, is contrary to our understanding of what "falling apart" means. But perceptive people never thought that the countries of Europe would throw themselves into each others' arms in the first place. Nevertheless, sufficient coherence has now been attained in the relations between them that it should be sustained.' Is that not a contradiction? What would one be sustaining? 'As much sympathy as possible between the European nations, without pretending that the French or Germans had abandoned the national character of their beliefs,' G. replied. 'It would be a disservice to believe that they could,' he added.

Should they not try to abandon them? I asked. 'No

individual can express a valid opinion on the matter. But there is no nation which would shed its own national opinions, image and beliefs. In this country, for instance, such beliefs are respectable and well-grounded.' Does 'closer union with Europe', allowing for doubt as to the meaning of the words, threaten those 'beliefs'? 'It would be over-sanguine to think that there is no danger of losing them. A good illustration is to be found in the development in Germany of a new Nazi ideology. I do not believe such a development could take place in England, but it is better not to say so.' Why? 'Because it would be tempting Providence,' G. replied.

And what of a Europe led by Germany? 'It depends what you mean. Take the average household in, say, Streatham. Let alone being "led by Germany", they don't even eat sauerkraut there.' (I misheard this, thinking G. had said that 'they don't even need sauerkraut there'. 'They don't need sauerkraut either,' G. declared with a laugh.) 'No German institution impinges on a normal household in Streatham,' he repeated. So such fears are a figment of feverish imaginations? 'They are unrealistic in relation to the lives of most Englishmen,' G. answered.

But it does not signify, said I, that such fears of 'domination', whether by Germany or Europe or what-ever, are without any substance. 'The only activity which has taken on a genuine European character at all is football,' G. said phlegmatically. Surely you don't mean that football alone possesses a European dimension? 'In terms of the numbers of people attracted to it being sufficient to qualify for such a designation, yes. Music and drama, philosophy and the fine arts have a European dimension too, but they are minute dimensions.' The worlds of Racine and Mozart, or Beethoven and Rembrandt, are of minute dimensions? 'They may be the one hope for the world, but they are of minute significance in terms of the numbers who care for them, especially in relation to the size of populations as a whole,' said G.

I get the clear impression that you regard the 'great debate about Europe' as so much cant and humbug, said I. 'But it is good cant and humbug on the whole, as opposed to bad cant and humbug. And better a shrill debate on "European values" than no debate at all.' Nevertheless, there is much about your position that surprises me. Is not the 'European Jew' an archetype? 'Is there such a thing as an archetypal Jew?' G. asked in return. 'Jews, wherever they are, have strong similarities, but is there such a category as "European Jews"? French Jews, for instance, have over the years distanced themselves from other Jews.'

Is there no 'European civilisation', then, of Jew and non-Jew alike, to be defended from barbarous encroachments upon it? 'There is no "civilisation" which prevails in every European territory to defend against the advent of barbarism', G. repeated. 'Individual countries manifest such "civilisation" in varying strengths. Take anti-semitism as an example. It reached a new and horrible height in Nazi Germany. But, marching alongside it, there was a degree of anti-semitism in France which was in some ways as bad. The French handed over their Jews to Germany with an enthusiasm which was indecent.'

The Germans, in particular, seem not to have been protected from evil-doing by their relative cultivation; Beethoven and Goethe did not stand in their way, said I. 'Culture is not a defence against barbarism. One merely hopes that cultivated people will not become barbarians themselves.' And there is not really any 'common European culture' either? 'No. To what extent could it be said to operate in Ireland, for example? The Irish have made substantial contributions to the world's culture: Wilde, Shaw and so on. But when an Irishman goes to prayer in his Catholic church, he does not offer up prayers to "European civilisation" or "European culture".'

The Pope certainly believes that there is such a thing as 'European', or at least 'Western', 'civilisation'. 'The Pope,' G. rejoined, 'is a special problem and I would rather not address it. Nevertheless, in order to maintain a decent level of morality some form of religious belief is better than none', he added. In particular, said I, the Pope addresses himself to something called 'European Christian civilisation'. 'Belief in a "European Christian civilisation" is an eccentricity,' G. declared briskly. But it played a significant part in the successful Papal crusade against communism in Eastern Europe? 'In the struggle against fanaticism it served as an argument, ironical as that might be.'

To return to the question of Germany, do you harbour any feelings that it is *sui generis* as a nation? 'I hope that it was unique in its demonstration of the Nazi horrors,' G. replied. 'Now the old type of hatreds are being redirected, principally against refugees who think they have found a safe haven there.' Did you have any feelings of awkwardness in being in Germany for the first time recently? 'Not of awkwardness, but feelings of distaste. There are, of course, certain Jews who at no time in their lives feel any special sense of Jewishness, and who can go to Germany without feelings of unease. I did not see or hear anything in Germany which manifested a Nazi attitude. But the whole atmosphere was, for me, heavy with the recall of what happened 50 years ago.'

That was in you, not in the atmosphere? 'It was in one's imagination, but it was also in the air.' What was in the air? 'I can describe it only as a Nazi sensation, or something which makes it uncomfortable for a self-respecting and firmly-admitted Jew to be in a country which threw Jewish children into gas-chambers, and inflicted extremes of humiliation on so many Jewish people. It is, in my judgment, a piece of excessive forgiveness for any Jew to visit Germany even now. On the other hand, it is also unreasonable not to forgive the Germans in the fullness of time.' Do you actually feel guilty at having stepped on to its soil? 'Not guilty, but it was a weakness on my part to have gone there.'

To what do you feel you gave way? 'I have given way to a willingness to forgive and forget which is possibly respectable but unreasonable.' I also take it, said I, that you would not have wanted to make a visit to Dachau or Belsen. 'I have sufficient imagination,' G. replied, 'not to want to inflict on myself the sight of such places.' Would it be reasonable for a Jew now to regret that Germany, as a nation, was not utterly destroyed, and that no one pronounced 'Carthago delenda est'? I asked. 'It is impossible for any Jew to establish a sensible reaction to Germany. But it must start with a willingness to reject recollections of what the Germans did to the Jews which intrude. That is not to say that the atrocities should be forgotten, but they should not be regarded as relevant to relations between Jews and Germans today.'

Yet you yourself were unable in Germany to keep such recollection at bay? 'The fact that I recalled the Nazi period does not invalidate my belief that it is a misfortune for everyone to recollect it.' Nevertheless, you are expecting a restraint from others, especially Jews, which you could not command in yourself. 'The whole history of morality is of people urging on others things which they themselves neither did nor believed,' said G. mischievously. 'The things that happened in the Nazi period are too compelling to be dismissed from the memory, too horrible to be forgotten. In fact, to forget them is unworthy. But I do not believe in continued retribution. Moreover, the fact that I have the feelings which I have about what the Germans did to the Jews does not make those feelings fit for general adoption. At no stage could I say that I am totally forgetful of the Nazi atrocities. But I would not allow my behaviour to be regulated by it in any serious fashion.'

But after your visit to Germany, don't you at all regret the position you took in the House of Lords on the War Crimes Bill? 'No. The bill related not to Germany, but to Britain. The position I took was that it was a folly, and a legal absurdity, for the British penal system to keep alive in Britain crimes committed 50 years ago.' As you kept those crimes alive in your own mind in Germany? 'No. The recall of these things in my mind was not of great importance to others. It is a different matter to espouse a national policy to pursue crimes 50 years old, and to resurrect national hatreds in this manner.'

To 'let bygones be bygones' is a different matter for the law than for the individual? 'It is. But one must accept that there are occasions when, for the individual too, common sense rightly displaces hatred and recollection of past injury. It is certainly not possible to acquiesce in the keeping alive of every national hatred. The sooner such hatreds are trodden underfoot the better.' Isn't that precisely the argument for 'European unity'? I asked. 'There are irresistible arguments for it,' G. replied, 'but they are not realistic.' If they are not realistic, is it not a snare and delusion to pursue such unity? 'It is not only unproductive but injurious to pursue it.' Such national hatreds will therefore remain? 'In some cases, no doubt. One sees it in

Northern Ireland, where hatred and prejudice are kept alive from no other motive than a desire to do so.'

There are also historical grounds for such hatred, said I. 'Historical ground is no ground. An animus should not be based on an historical ground.' It is so based for the Jews, as you have revealed. Why is it right for the Jews, and wrong for the Irish? 'But it is not right. The Irish example is the best example of the evil that comes from memories that do not fade. Such memories are memories not only of what happened but what people imagine happened. I am perfectly willing to let people have the same attitude as the Jews have to those who have done them wrong, but it should be associated with a readiness to forget as soon as possible. The Nazi outrages are too recent. Most of us lived through them. Memories of Cromwell, however, are an insufficient justification for today's assassinations in Northern Ireland.' Nevertheless, I repeated, you too felt dogged by the shadows of the past. 'That is an exaggeration. I became conscious of something in the atmosphere. If you find yourself socialising with people who you think might in the past have humiliated Jews or killed Jewish children, it is very difficult to dismiss the sense of it from the social atmosphere. That is relevant. I was well received. But even so, overhanging the whole situation, there was bound to be a recollection of what happened only 50 years ago.'

It seems to me, said I, that you are struggling with two conflicting emotions: to be free of prejudice on the one hand, and not to compromise your fidelity to your Jewishness on the other. 'Are they conflicting? How do they conflict?' G. asked sharply. On the one hand, I replied, you do not wish to be swayed by your emotions on the subject, and on the other your sense of yourself as a Jew makes it difficult for reason alone to command your responses. 'The virtue is in not wanting, or not being willing, to be affected by such emotion. It is important for a Jew not to have deep hatreds. Deep hatreds are useless and unrewarding emotions.' But it is not wrong to claim that it is often difficult for a Jew to keep such emotion at bay? 'No. It is a natural situation. I would not wish to retain any hostility to anyone. But there are times when it is hard to observe that rule, whether in regard to the Nazis or to blatant anti-semitism in England.'

Did you vote against the War Crimes Bill in part to show that you were not susceptible to the supposedly Jewish instinct for 'revenge'? 'I have never identified such an instinct in Jews, except occasionally where you might meet it in the relatives of those who were murdered in the Holocaust, or in the emotions of the Eichmann trial. Even in such instances it was not very well defined, and was as much an assertion of Jewish self-respect as of revenge.' But did you consciously try to avoid creating any impression in the debate about war crimes that you could be actuated by 'Jewish revenge'? 'I do not think it is really a Jewish attribute,' G. repeated. 'I hope it is not. Nor do I have any Christian friends who believe I am moved by a desire to avenge myself on them for what has been done to the Jews,' G. added with a laugh. You didn't kill any 'Jerries' in the war? 'I never killed anybody. But I was involved in a small way as an anti-aircraft gunner in bringing down aeroplanes. However, no anti-aircraft gunner ever thinks he is killing anyone,' said G.

What do you think were Winston Churchill's real feelings during the war about the predicament of the Jews? 'He saw the threat to them from the Nazis. But he was not concerned to protect or defend the Jews as such. What they were suffering was an added make-weight.' What do you mean? 'Churchill was to some extent influenced by the Nazis' anti-Jewish activities, but not to any very great extent. He had sufficient motivation in his prosecution of the war from the threat to England and the British Empire.'

Has it puzzled you that the railway lines along which millions of Jews travelled to their deaths were not bombed, whether by the British or anyone else? 'I do not think British military policy, or any other military policy, was affected by a consideration of helping or not helping the Jews, but of advancing the military cause.' But is it not cause for despair that the supply of 'Jewish transports' was never interrupted by bombs? 'Unless one knows more of the logistics which were involved, one cannot say what diversion of military resources would have been needed. It is not clear that what would have been achieved by bombing the camps, or the railway lines, would even have been to the benefit of the Jews.'

Nevertheless, I persisted, some Jews, perhaps most Jews, see it as a particular sin of the war that the attempt was not made. 'Just as there are Jews who think that the world is not good enough for them,' said G. with sudden asperity, 'so there are some Jews who pick on the relatively trivial or insignificant fact that the railway lines to the concentration camps were not bombed.' How can you say it was trivial? 'It was trivial by the side of the general policy to win the war. The central requirement for the Jews was that Nazism was defeated.' Yes, but trivial? 'I think it is a side-issue whether the Allies took this or that particular step in their conduct of the war. I am sure that it was not from conscious hostility to the Jews that the step was not taken.' Perhaps, said I, but I still do not see how you can call the step, had it been taken, 'insignificant', or suggest that Jews who remain bewildered by the failure are wrong.

'As you know,' said G., unmoved, 'it does not take long for Jews to find a grievance. In a way it is responsible for their survival,' he added.

You have never been tempted to pacifism by the miseries of the war? 'No. Pacifism is a melodramatic demonstration,' G. replied. Of what? I asked. 'Of an allegedly superior moral attitude.' Is it not morally superior? 'It is obviously unrealistic,' G. replied briefly. Advice to 'turn-the-other-cheek' is then no moral maxim? 'It is a phrase which conjures up a sense of moral superiority and which it is better not to use.' Yet there are many who set great store by it, said I. 'That is because it is inherent in the whole of the Christian doctrine. But it is not inherent in Jewish doctrine. To that extent, Jewish doctrine is superior.'

So if the Christian wishes to believe in 'turning the other cheek', that is up to him? Is that what you are saying. 'In a sense that is my view.' Such a morality does not embody a universal value? 'It would have universal value if one could establish that it had universal application. That it has not. Most people do not settle their grievances by turning the other cheek. It is a highly civilised injunction, and we owe it to the Christians to acknowledge and respect it. But it could not, even in the best of circumstances, be practised by every man and woman. The likelihood is that in the heat of emotion it would not be practised at all, if it was practised by anyone. If you become engaged in a private conflict and someone hits you in the eye, your first reaction is not to say, "Hit me in the other one".'

It is a maxim only for the superlatively noble? 'No. It has value as a moral maxim like any other, such as that enjoining you to "love your neighbour as yourself". If your neighbour's rottweiler is in your garden and about to tear you to pieces, it is difficult to operate this maxim,' G. said. At which he began to laugh until there were tears in his eyes; his laughter was infectious, and it was some time before we could resume.

But are you saying that Jewish morality is superior because Jews do not believe in 'turning the other cheek'? 'Not quite that. The Jews, contrary to what is said of them, do not in general pursue vengeance. The best statement of Jewish morality is in the service for the Day of Atonement, in which Jews are enjoined to do a small number of things, but enjoined not to do a large number. In that respect, Judaism is rather unique.' But Christians, said I, might argue that because Jews do not believe as an article of faith in turning the other cheek they are therefore predisposed to be vengeful. 'That is not so,' said G. severely, 'while Christians, for their parts, espouse a doctrine with high moral content but one which could be practised only by a very small number of people.' Your objection to the maxim, then, is practical not philosophical? 'It is practical and philosophical,' G. replied.

8

The Law, Justice
and Injustice

I said to G. that I had myself been called to the Bar but had not been able to face the prospect of being a lawyer. Did you actually *want* to be a lawyer? I asked him. Why did you do it? 'I arrived at the rational conclusion that there was no valid alternative,' G. answered. 'I needed a profession which would, above all, ensure my continuance. It had to provide a living, a tolerable living; I had no expectation that I would come by any wealth from its practice. My choice also had to satisfy several other criteria. I required a profession which entailed an academic background of some sort. I did not want a profession into which one could walk without effort, a profession in which the whole world was a competitor. It had also to have an intrinsic interest, and be a profession which provided comradeship.

'Lawyers can and should be good friends. I do not mean by that every lawyer is your friend, or that you should seek to make him so. But it is a profession which admits friendship and almost obliges it. A lawyer who is not on good terms with his colleagues is a disadvantage to his clients.' Would you not rather have gone to the Bar? 'I had a choice. Without being cynical, my principal objection was that as a barrister all my customers would have had to be solicitors. Nor do I regret that I did not belong to a body so resistant to advice, narrow-minded, bigoted and hostile to change as the Bar. Its refusal to accept reform and its clinging to privilege and tradition are not recommendations.'

But is such objection, however forcefully you put it, really a sufficient ground for you to have chosen years ago to be a solicitor rather than to go to the Bar? 'It was a sufficient ground, but one of several. First of all, I had to face up to the fact that at the time I had no firm [financial] support. I am sufficiently vain to believe that I would have been a success at the Bar. I am a pretty good lawyer, not without gifts of oratory, and it would not have taken me long to build up a practice. But it is also a profession to which you must sell yourself body and soul. The great advantage of being a solicitor – an advantage which has emerged, and was not something which I anticipated – is that you can simultaneously do a large number of other things.'

You are telling me that, despite your 'gifts of oratory' and other gifts besides, you have no regrets at missing the 'allure' of the Bar? 'No regrets at all,' G. cheerfully replied. 'The so-called alluring side of the Bar is, in any event, meretricious. There is a great deal of humbug in it. It must also be wrong,' G. added, 'that success in any legal issue can depend – not necessarily so, but it often does – on the choice of advocate.'

Despite these objections to the life of the Bar, said I, your skills and persona could have made you one of the great luminaries of the Bench. 'Maybe. But that is a position I would never have sought. I joined a profession from which I could not have been promoted in that fashion. It offered no such risk. I would ten times rather have been Chairman of the Arts Council than a Lord Justice of Appeal.' Nevertheless, I wonder whether, since to be a solicitor is to be a member of the 'junior' profession in the law, your harsh criticisms of the Bar are not actuated by some kind of resentment? 'They do not flow from any sense of resentment.' And of the Bench? 'My objection to the English judiciary is, in a word, that it is class-ridden.'

Yet, with your capacity to assess argument swiftly, and deliver yourself lucidly of your opinions, you possess judicial skills yourself. 'Whether I possess such skills or not has not weighed in my objections. The life of a judge is of insufferable tedium. He is required to listen to every idiot who comes before him and who can speak as long as he likes.' But as a judge you would have had the power to cut him off in mid-flow. 'In which case, he would have gone to the Court of Appeal, complaining that his argument was "cut short by Mr Justice Goodman", who "would not listen" to him.' Despite all this, I said, you want to give solicitors the right of audience before the higher courts, so that they can add further to the tedium? 'That,' replied G., dismissively, 'stems from my belief that there should be a unitary profession. I am hostile to the Bar because of its disinclination to allow solicitors to perform their functions as lawyers, and to plead for their clients.' You think it is an artificial restraint of trade? 'Yes, quite.'

What qualities are required of a judge? I asked. 'A normal understanding of human beings is the vital requirement. Most of the judges are very middle-class, have been to public schools and attended one of the "ancient universities". They cannot think as an ordinary working-class person thinks.' Does it matter? 'Any judicial system should have a sufficiently popular basis to enable the ordinary man and woman to think the system not entirely remote from them,' G. replied. But surely you are not saying that class origin should be a criterion of judicial selection, when it is not so in other professions? 'The requirement to judge someone outside your class, and even to send him to jail, does not arise in other professions,' said G. Nevertheless, your criticism of the judiciary could be regarded as rather populist, said I. 'It is a serious shortcoming in a judge,' G. retorted, 'that he cannot readily understand every other class. He may be able readily to understand the drunkenness and adultery, say, of fellow-members of his class, but that is an insufficient qualification.'

What must the judge understand of the working class? 'He must understand,' G. replied, 'the relevance of poverty in everyday life, of not having a roof over one's head, of sleeping in the open air. He has to understand the whole gamut of lower-class requirements.' Are you saying that judges do not understand any of this? 'Many judges do, but a great many do not,' answered G. But what guarantee is there that solicitors on the Bench would understand better? 'The choice available is from 3,000 members of the Bar against 60,000 solicitors. Your chance of alighting upon a solicitor who is an understanding human being is twenty times as large.'

But have you not known wise as well as inadequate or even wicked judges? 'Yes, I have, and not many who were wicked. I would, however, have regarded Lord Goddard as wicked on the strength of some of his summings-up in criminal cases; in civil cases, there is no judge I would have preferred. His summing-up in the Bentley murder trial, for example, was appalling.' Why? 'He introduced irrelevant considerations into it in order to persuade the jury to bring in a verdict of murder.' What about Lord Denning and his remark that Sir Leon Brittan was a 'German Jew' interfering with 'English law'. 'Lord Denning,' G. replied, 'is an unfortunate example of a man who built up a reputation on sand.' That could be actionable, said I. 'I do not care if it is,' G. roundly replied. 'It is characteristic of the English legal profession that it should set a man like Lord Denning on a pedestal. In the matter of precedent, he went further than any living individual to destroy it. He is basically a kind man, but that does not make you a good judge in itself, even if it goes some way towards it.'

Is your objection to Denning that he exercised his discretion as a judge too arbitrarily, that he became too much a legislator, disguised or undisguised? 'One part of law-making is, quite properly, judicial utterance, and judges must have discretion in order to arrive at appropriate judgments in each case. But it should be more carefully regulated.' It is not the judges' role to enforce morals? 'They are not there to impose their moral notions upon mankind. It is unreal, however, to expect a man to be separated from his ethical beliefs when he becomes a judge. This makes it the more important to scrutinise closely candidates for high legal office before their elevation.' What do you mean by 'scrutinise'? 'Take a good look at their life-styles, who their friends are, even what their politics are.'

That has an inquisitorial and oppressive ring to it, said I. 'You have to do it, just as when you appoint a secretary you would reasonably inquire into an individual's background. Moreover, the problem lies not so much with those who are appointed judges as those who are not.' Is not my prior question about the judge's moral function a bigger issue? 'It is not that big. Any judgment in the criminal law is an assertion of morality. Anyone convicted of theft, for example, is being subjected to one of the Ten Commandments. When a judge carries out his ordinary function under the criminal law the necessity of enforcing a morality is supposed. A warning to an accused not to steal and not to assault his fellow-men contains the moral code.' But is it the judge's business to go so far as to try to suppress vice? 'If the legislators have not performed their task,' G. replied, 'I do not mind a reserve team doing it for them. But I am not so much concerned about the judges' right, as their capacity, to do it. If you sit down at a dinner-table with half a dozen judges, you would be shocked at the reactionary nature of their views.' In respect to what? 'For example, in their attitudes towards everyday affairs like homosexuality.'

But 'reactionary' could be said to be too inexplicit and too easy a term of abuse. What do you mean by it? 'I mean,' G. replied, 'that they are constrained by notions which are out of date or more generally inappropriate for a modern society.' To what are you referring specifically? I asked. 'To a determination, for example, to dress themselves up in Jacobean costume.' That is surely a superficial symptom of reaction? 'It is a symptom.' And how would the 'progressive' judge of the future behave if he were to earn your approval? 'It would require such a leap of the imagination on my part that I am not sure any good purpose would be served in conjecturing it,' G. replied with a laugh. Perhaps, but someone might say that if you want the judiciary to be 'progressive' you should explain in what ways. 'That is as if a zoologist were being asked to explain to a snake why it should shed its skin.'

Are you saying that every judge is a reactionary? 'I am not saying that every judge is a reactionary, but there is a sufficient number of them who are.' But this is true in every walk of life and in every profession, said I. 'The fact that greengrocers are by tradition reactionary is less socially important than that judges are reactionary. If my greengrocer phones Mrs Hargreaves [G.'s housekeeper] saying, "I have heard that Lord Goodman has socialist opinions, and I will not deliver his order for greengages", that would not be a significant occurrence.' And to weed out judges whose opinions are analogous to those of your supposed greengrocer, you want to see a body of inquisitors at work? The question was brushed aside. 'Judicial appointments,' G. declared, 'are officially made by the Lord Chancellor, but unofficially it is understood to be on the recommendation of a team of advisers. I asked the Lord Chancellor in the House of Lords whether he was satisfied by this system. He said he was very satisfied, since he knew the people [sc. the leading candidates from the Bar] better than others did. I replied, "You know *some* of the people. That makes the situation far worse." '

You are not suggesting that the condition of the judiciary is irremediable? 'Nothing is irremediable. Any institution which can be changed by changing its personnel can be changed, even if it takes years. Indeed, the present Lord Chancellor is more discriminating and fair-minded than his predecessors in this regard.' But do you not have any anxiety, at a time when many other British institutions are being put in question, that your criticisms of the judiciary might merely be destructive? 'I do not think that constructive suggestions – that judges be more carefully selected, for example – can be considered destructive. I want the judiciary to change and improve.' But by belabouring the judges as 'reactionaries' you don't fear to impugn the majesty of the law? I asked. 'The very word majesty is suspect. It presupposes that the judges have a majesty to preserve. They are conscious of their own dignity, but in the position they hold they have to be. What they have to preserve is the integrity of the law, its simplicity – if any simplicity still exists – and its fundamental justice, all of which are in doubt.'

Certain kinds of criticism do not add to their 'dignity', said I. 'I am not concerned with adding to their dignity. They themselves preserve a pretty stout attitude which certainly maintains their dignity. I would not want to alter that. Judges should be held in respect.' Do not flummery, ceremony and even Jacobean costume have a positive purpose? 'They have a positive purpose. The mistake the judges make is to think that they add something to the dignity of the law. I do not think that being dressed up in Jacobean costume adds either to their dignity or to the dignity of the law. What adds to their dignity is total integrity and solid learning.'

You are saying that by these and the other means you have indicated the law will then be held in due respect? 'I should hope so. Where law is not respected and stands in questionable estimation, that is a very bad thing. One does not want reverence to the law to the extent of feeling obliged to drop to one's knees when the word is mentioned. In my case,' G. added cheerfully, 'I would have difficulty in getting up.'

But surely miscarriages of justice are a more important question than the class provenance or costume of the judges? 'Miscarriages of justice,' said G., 'are more than a part attributable to the class nature of the judiciary.' You sound like a Marxist, said I. 'I don't mind sounding like a Marxist in this respect. The incidence of class in this country is under-rated.' But it is a very reductive argument to refer your entire criticism of the judiciary ultimately to issues of class? Is it nothing but their class provenance that is wrong with the judges?

'One important matter,' G. replied, 'is that there is engendered in them, by training and background, an unthinking attitude to life and a feeling of infallibility about their judgments. One of the worst qualities of the English judiciary is the belief that it is infallible. This is best illustrated by the iron determination with which it clings to error. When it is obvious to everyone but themselves that a conclusion they have reached is erroneous, it would require a battalion of guards to remove them from their position. It is not true of all judges, but it is true of some who are very senior. The magnitude of their errors is compounded by the difficulty of getting these judges removed.'

Is there a particular kind of judicial fallibility which you have in mind? 'There is a certain kind of *fallible judge*,' G. replied. 'He has been brought up in the belief that the English legal system is the best in the world. This is a dangerous belief to hold, and one unlikely to respond to an invitation to admit the possibility of error. If you were similarly to believe that our traffic system was the best in the world, it would be one of the most startling beliefs of modern times. But with such beliefs it is very hard to put things to rights, since those who hold them believe that critics are attempting to improve upon perfection. In the case of the judiciary and the judicial system, this is a silly belief and one which could only be maintained by those who were in ignorance of the true situation.'

If all this is so, are the defects of which you complain long-standing or relatively recent? 'They were immanent in the system from the beginning,' G. replied. 'They have become worse in recent times, as particular errors have been repeated, and, in some cases, particular judges have become more established in their mistaken positions.' What particular errors are you referring to? 'Cases, for example, where disturbing and even outrageous judgments have had to be reversed, cases in which there have been clearly wrong assessments of fact and wrong assessments of expert evidence. They are all faults which would have been eradicated by a judiciary more perceptive, even if less learned.' Are these errors of principle or of ill-functioning institutions? 'They have, in essence, a professional origin. When you are first introduced into the legal system you encounter the assumption – a fundamental symptom of the reactionary attitude – that no better system than the common law ever existed. Such a proposition is generally asserted by those who have known no other, but who are not daunted from making the claim by the fact that they have nothing with which to compare it.'

If there are the errors you speak of, this assumption of superiority surely cannot be a sufficient explanation of them, said I? 'It is a large explanation of them,' G. replied. 'The same sort of malady afflicts the English medical profession, which also believes itself to be the best in the world.' Is there no ground for it? 'To entertain it without qualm,' G. replied, 'you would have to be blindfold and wearing ear-plugs.' Are you really saying, I asked, that when the luckless defendant stands before a judge it is the latter's views about the superior quality of the English legal system which puts the former at the greatest risk? 'It gives massive support to his erroneous views, and is inherent in them,' G. persisted.

What if the defendant's real problem is that he has had his confession extorted from him by the police, say? Is that not a graver matter? 'It is itself a horror, but it should be a self-correcting horror. It is when you get a judge with a belief in the combined infallibility of the judicial system and the police system that the danger of injustice is increased. The British race,' G. continued, 'is raw material as good as you would find anywhere in the world on which to build a legal and police system. But the various processes to which that raw material is subjected are corrupting.'

In what respects? 'One of the worst faults in relation to the police, and to a lesser extent in relation to the judiciary, is xenophobia. Large numbers of policemen – not all – have a built-in suspicion and dislike of what they call "foreigners".' Including the Irish? I said. 'Very much so,' said G. Are you suggesting that this is a principal reason for miscarriages of justice involving Irish defendants? 'Precisely. The whole atmosphere is often weighed against them. It is true that the Irish are committing totally unjustifiable outrages both against their fellow Irishmen and against others. But in a situation where such outrages are particularly associated with one community the chances that members of that community will be subject to injustice, rather than to disinterested judgment, are very high. They are highest when those who are judging them entertain xenophobic feelings about them.'

None of these flaws, said I, has to do with defects of legal principle as such: they are all matters of blindness or prejudice of one kind and another. 'There is also the question of the essential nature of English law and its foundations, which I believe in some ways to be inherently wrong.' You are not saying that the whole system of precedent is flawed? 'It would require a revolutionary attitude on the part of law-makers, judges and prac-titioners of law to recognise that the system of precedent is not only fallible and unsystematic but also dangerous,' G. declared. 'It also adds enormously to the cost of litigation that anything which might relate to the instant case has to be read to the judge. It is clear that, apart from anything else, this involves considerable time and expense.' Do you mean that there is something vitiated at the very heart of the English legal system? ' "Vitiated" is putting it too strongly. Generally, the system of precedent functions quite easily. You can find a precedent in a large number of cases which fits closely. But there is a specialised number of cases where you have to search hard for an appropriate precedent, and even have to invent one.'

Are you denying that the English system of precedent is superior to the Napoleonic code, for instance? 'It is not superior. Its principal flaw lies in its absence of certainty, where you do not know what the law is until a suitable precedent has been discovered. Moreover, very often a case is in practice decided not by precedent but by the individual judge's own thinking. This is supposedly wrong jurisprudentially.' Is it wrong? 'I think it is wrong. It is wrong above all for judges to pretend that their decision in a particular case is supported by precedent when it is not. You may not arrive at any *flamingly* inaccurate or unfair judgments, but quite often you arrive at inaccurate and unfair judgments. That is why I prefer a system of principle to a system of precedent.'

Yet you criticised Lord Denning for having done much to destroy the system of precedent? Ought you not to be grateful to him for having done everyone a service, if the system is as you say it is? 'If he did us a service, he did it by accident,' G. replied tartly. 'It was not a deliberate service. He is a very vain man. He pretends to respect, and even to reverence, the rule of law as established by precedent but reveres nothing except his own opinion.' But if precedent is so dangerous, why object so strongly to the individual who has undermined it? 'I do not think that he thinks it a dangerous thing. He is a man working from a quite different position from mine. He professes to believe firmly in precedent, but when it comes to it he does not believe in it at all. The whole thing is hypocrisy.' Nevertheless, you could still be grateful to him for not believing in precedent if it has the defects you mention, I ventured. 'I have not the slightest reason to be grateful for his muddle-headed actions. If he has done something which is not as disastrously wrong as is usual, that is an entire accident.'

From what you have said, I take your position to be that there are substantive defects in the law which are compounded, among other things, by the nature of the 'raw material' of which the judiciary is composed? 'It is the intellectual material which is suspect,' said G. Are you saying that judges are stupid? 'Not so much stupid as persuaded early in their careers at the Bar that things which are basically wrong are entirely right,' G. answered.

Is there the same kind of mistaken belief, as you would see it, in the virtues of other British institutions? 'The belief in the infallibility of one British institution can very easily spread over into others. Anyone who believed that the British parliamentary system was perfect would himself deserve to be removed to an institution.'

Could you envisage a future tyranny in this country which rested upon such beliefs in the perfection of British institutions? 'The risk relates only to the tyrannies of particular groups of people. There is no doubt that in selecting the exhibits for the Royal Academy summer show each year there must be an element of tyranny. It is the result of ceding excessive power to any one person or group of persons. Moreover, all learning tyrannises ignorance,' G. added. You are not kept awake at night over our so-called 'elective dictatorship'? 'Provided that there is a fair system of election, a parliamentary democracy, despite its imperfections, is the best system of government mankind has ever produced. It is not a tyranny to cede to a particular group power that derives from the votes of a majority of the people.' It was a minority of the electorate, said I, which returned Mrs Thatcher to office three times. 'With any system of election you must allow for a number of people who do not opt into it. If you do not get a sufficient proportion of the electorate participating, the system is not working. But most of us are fervent democrats who believe that rule by the choice of a majority, even if it is not perfect, is the best rule that can be had.'

Is not the judiciary, in the light of your criticisms of it, the embodiment of an undemocratic tradition? 'Unless the judiciary has sufficient, and even considerable, powers, it cannot perform its functions. That is acceptable on the basis that it is not entirely corrupt, and will go out of its way to give what it thinks is a fair verdict. I do not think such powers affect the democratic process.' But surely, if the judiciary is as 'class-ridden' as you claim, it must have a negative bearing on the democratic process, said I. 'Only in the sense that class is embedded in the entire social order, so that you expect to find it everywhere,' said G.

Is there a natural arrogance, or congenital superiority complex, in the English? 'No. Ingrained ideas about the superiority of British institutions are fed to children, especially of the upper middle class, at an early age. These are less powerful than they were, because the notion of empire has been much reduced. The idealised view of an India governed entirely by a handful of civil servants, and in which unarguable justice was meted out to every Indian, could only have been maintained by an unshakeable conviction of British excellence.'

Are you saying that this 'conviction of British excellence' has declined? 'It is a conviction which has suffered in recent years. Now no one has the confidence in British products, for example, which they had before. However, there is no doubt that products such as HP sauce retain their excellent qualities.' But, as far as the law is concerned, is the belief in its excellence and infallibility also diminishing? 'This weakness is still very substantial at the top of the profession, even if it is somewhat less noticeable. To a degree it is self-correcting. Some of the individuals most convinced of their infallibility have gone, and many swollen heads have been reduced by several millimetres. This is clear evidence that something has improved. Nevertheless, most of the judiciary continues to surrender to a national self-conceit of terrifying dimensions.' It may terrify the innocent defendant, said I, but whom else should it frighten? 'All potential defendants,' G. replied. Such fears might have their positive aspect, said I. 'You might as well argue,' G. retorted, 'that if no one believes that he will get a fair trial, it might lead to a reduction in crime.'

Do you think that people in authority in Britain, including the police, are growing less scrupulous? 'I do. It might seem a facile explanation, but it is because of deficiencies in education, and more damaging, in moral education. People are not being educated to behave well either at school or at home.' Is this a problem of serious proportion? 'It is certainly serious.' Together with what you regard as the defects of the judiciary, could a lack of scruple among the police be said to have 'undermined' the law? 'It is certainly gravely deficient on account of these factors. A want of public confidence in the operation of the law now extends, perhaps unfairly in some instances, to the behaviour of the police.'

But isn't the problem of the volume of crime, and of the nature of the crimes which some people are increasingly prepared to commit against others, much more serious? Killings at the slightest provocation, kickings to death, rapes of old women and such like? 'I cannot make anything of such crimes. I can only surmise that there is a greater number of deranged people than there ever was before. When a man is suddenly attacked and beaten to death by an individual he has never before set eyes on, it opens up a terrifying prospect.' There is even, said I, increasing violence, some of it of the greatest callousness, being directed in Britain at young children and animals. 'It is one of the great myths that the British love animals and children,' G. rejoined. 'No community demonstrates greater cruelty to both these species.' Has it reached the point where no punishment could 'fit the crime'? 'It has not yet reached that point. On the whole, hanging a man would satisfy most desires for punishment,' G. jocularly added. But not long ago, said I, a man was robbed at knife-point in Reading of £20 while he was having an epileptic fit. What punishment could fit that? 'You do not try to equate a punishment to the heinousness of a crime,' G. answered sternly. 'If a man murders someone, that murder is the crime. If he subsequently cuts up his victim into pieces and eats him, that does not make the crime more serious.' What does it do? 'It makes the crime more horrible,' G. answered.

'Mark you,' he continued, 'you have to bear in mind that press coverage of crime is as never before.' In the past, the impact of a Crippen or Christie was felt by the public for years, said I. 'That is true. Murders pass now with little effect. Serious crime no longer provokes a degree of response which is compatible with its gravity.' But I also do not recall in the past the gratuitous and easily provoked brutality of much of today's violence, said I. 'I do not recall it either. But even allowing that past crimes were less heinous than the present lot, they were also not publicised as they are now. Serious crimes are now both more frequent and better advertised. "Sadism" is a word which was not used as much in my youth as it is now.

Now it provides a convenient if unscientific explanation for dreadful happenings which could not be otherwise explained. "Sadist" is merely a word, but a convenient word.'

Do you not find an alarming degree of public resignation, or even insouciance, about today's passing brutalities? 'There is an acceptance by the public of a level of crime which would not have been accepted previously. This is particularly so in the case of sex crimes. How far it is the result of more compassionate punishments I do not know. I have never believed that hanging or other violent forms of punishment deterred anyone. But that belief must be qualified by the fact that, in the absence of such punishment, violent crimes take place to a greater extent than previously.'

Are you implying that you are now in favour of the death penalty? 'There is something so inherently horrible about the death penalty that I would need a great deal of convincing that that is the way to save the lives of others, if such an outcome could be achieved by such methods. But I am not saying that today it would be impossible to convince me. I am veering towards that conviction, but I do not *want* to arrive at it. There is certainly a public mood that more condign punishment would produce more effective results.' Would it? 'I do not know. But if you are going to take extreme measures, you must take those which are effective. It is probable that you would only have to boil one person in oil to make a powerful impact, but unfortunately – or fortunately – civilised nations prevent it.'

In which case, given the volume of crime of all kinds, the prisons must continue to fill to overflowing? 'There is no solution in locking people up when the accommodation is inadequate to house them. More thought will have to be given to alternative methods of punishment. The difficulty is that to satisfy everyone that their concerns are being taken into account, the various objects of punishment – principally those of deterrence and retribution – must continue to be addressed.' What alternatives to custodial sentences would you advocate? 'Fining people,' G. replied, 'can be, in many circumstances, a completely adequate punishment. Deprivation of privileges can also serve. To deprive a small boy who has been causing trouble of his right to go to a football match is, in his mind, a severe penalty.' Could not such punishments be extended to, say, deprivation of certain civic rights? 'It should be tried. Such a notion has not had sufficiently extensive tests to make a judgment. If you took away an individual's passport as a punishment it would not necessarily serve as a deterrent in every case. But if you took away the right to go to the cinema,' G. added, 'it might operate with a larger minority.'

In seventeenth-century Florence, a person declared by the magistrates to be a *bandito* lost his right to carry out legal transactions or to open a bank account. 'Those are middle-class penalties,' G. declared. 'You could not prevent crime by preventing the criminal from buying a copy of *The Times*.' But is not the principle which is embodied in depriving someone of his driving licence a good one, and one which could be extended to other civic rights? 'Perhaps. But in all punishments you have to touch an individual where it affects him most. If an individual set upon hooliganising the continent has to stay in Blackburn rather than going to watch his team play, he will be left foaming at the mouth.' He would be likely to be foaming at the mouth in any event, I said. 'For different reasons,' said G. 'In one case, he would be foaming at the mouth in order to demonstrate his unalterable hostility to his adversaries. In Blackburn, it would be because he had been prevented from getting at them. The latter is a better kind of foaming.'

Nevertheless, it is hard to find 'condign' forms of punishment other than the loss of liberty which are both effective and humane, said I. 'It is. But society will have to find methods of punishment which do not involve the present levels of incarceration, since the entire land cannot be filled with prisons. It might be appropriate, in some circumstances, to issue ration-books which prevented the holders of them from purchasing more than a limited amount of consumer goods. One can think of a number of imaginative ways of making people suffer.' No doubt, I said, but they are not being much discussed. 'Because such matters are largely dealt with by a Home Office which is not equipped to deal with them.'

But how is it, I asked, that when a bill was introduced into the House of Commons in an attempt to make parents responsible for the delinquencies of their children, it was laughed to scorn? 'Because it was an absurdity,' G. replied. Why? Is it not ethically sound that parents should be vested with moral and legal responsibility for the misconduct in their community of their own offspring, if they are minors still living at home? How can the social or civic order function without such responsibility? 'There is no case which is uniform in relation to every parent. Moreover, by the time that a boy or girl is old enough to be dealt with by the law it is right that the parents should be left out of it.'

Is it then wrong to impose upon parents responsibility for the conduct of their children? 'It is not wrong in this sense: if a child is too young to answer to the law, too young to compensate those who have suffered from his actions, and too young to rectify what he has done, it is right that someone should answer for them. But what if the child's parents are living apart? Do you visit the responsibility on the resident parent alone?' G. asked. Such questions, said I, may not be easy to answer. Nevertheless, it surely cannot be ethically wrong to attempt to fix some legal blame for the misconduct of the child upon its parents? 'It is *practically* wrong to do so,' G. replied swiftly. 'In cases of divorce or separated parents, it might have been the influence of a parent who has left the home which is responsible for what has happened. There are many other equal difficulties which can be imagined in the application of such a measure. On balance, it is better to leave the responsibility where it now falls.'

To many, that would sound merely like another admission that the problem of crime in general is beyond solution, said I. 'It is soluble only in the long term. To school people in morality is a very long-term project. But it will not be achieved by elderly gentlemen in horsehair wigs and flannelette gowns sitting six feet above ground level, because they will not produce a serious change in anything.' Nor, I said, will much moral benefit flow from 'privatising' the prisons. 'Privatising the prisons offends me greatly. The whole essence of a prison is that it is a place where people are kept under restraint by the ultimate threat of violence. It is impossible decently to delegate that threat to private persons.' The threat of violence? I do not follow, said I. 'In a prison, there is an unspoken understanding on all sides that those in control are entitled ultimately to resort to violence.' To beat prisoners on the head? 'To coerce them in some form, to push them, to restrain them. That threat must be involved.'

There are more powerful objections, said I. Civic society rests upon an implied social contract, under which the individual citizen delegates to the state the obligation of protecting him and administering an impartial system of justice, while he surrenders his right to protect himself and, *in extremis*, to take the law into his own hands. To privatise the prisons is for the state to break the social contract. 'This is true. I view the whole process which is underway with distaste, but above all because it is creating a situation in which people are seeking to make profit for themselves from the incarceration of others. The proposal would have been defeated if it had come before the House of Lords.'

Is your sense of justice Jewish in any sense that has meaning? 'A balanced sense of justice is universal,' G. replied. 'The only difference between a Jewish and a non-Jewish – or, if you like, a *goyishe* – sense of justice is that in the former case there might be a stronger determination to see justice done. But I do not think my sense of justice is stronger than David Astor's, for example.' Isn't he of Jewish origin himself? 'I do not know,' G. replied. 'But I would take him as a model citizen. Many would say that he was a "leftie" or a "softie" and so forth. But in my estimation he is a prototype of what a just man ought to be.'

Do Jews become lawyers for more reasons than that their mothers want it? Is a desire to 'serve justice' among them? 'Jews become lawyers for the innumerable reasons which make any person choose the law as a profession. A desire to "serve justice" may be among them. But in general they become lawyers as they might become chiropodists,' G. replied with a laugh. That cannot be so of you, said I; there is much that I have heard you say during our conversations which has echoes of the Torah. 'It would be ridiculous to suggest that, having read the Torah, it did not have an influence upon me.' In the Torah, I continued, truth is held 'not to be found in merchants or traders', Jews are enjoined to oppose the evils of acquisitiveness, not to misuse their wealth, to be benevolent towards the needy, to 'take care lest there be a wicked thought in your heart', and so on. Even the detail of some of the things you have said earlier coincides with Torah rules and prohibitions, for example that which forbids the creation of a monopoly in the basic necessities of life. 'All these biblical utterances have my approbation. But if I hold any views which are similar to them, it derives more from an instinctive than a conscious knowledge of them.' The Torah, contrary to the expectations of some, said I, even has stricter prohibitions against usury than against outright theft, let alone injunctions to give away a fixed proportion of one's wealth to the needy.

'Judaism has enjoined upon us a degree of kindness and benevolence almost impossible of attainment,' responded G., with a twinkle in his eye. 'I could give you a list of prominent Jews living nearby on whom you could call on your way home, and ask how many of them conduct themselves in accord with such requirements. Most universal moral codes prescribe a pattern of behaviour which it is unlikely that the great mass of mankind will observe.' Nevertheless, a moral code has been inherited by Jews, of which they have what you called an 'instinctive knowledge'? 'Yes, but to an even greater extent the same moral code has been disinherited by Jews.' Have you not been aware of practising, or attempting to practise, a moral code while acting as a lawyer? 'I am often aware that any other decision than the one I have reached would be immoral,' G. replied.

Yet much of your work, I suppose, involves not the pursuit of any moral ideal but mere practicalities, seeking the *via media*, or getting other people off the hook? 'It involves,' G. said with faint irritation, 'fulfilling my duty as a lawyer. I am not out for moral perfection, because the legal system does not admit of it. What you have to do is to find a sensible compromise between justice and morality.' And neither is attainable in any perfect state? 'That is certainly so.'

[9]

Objections to the Media

I said that I wanted to talk about the press and the other
media, at which G. shrugged and said 'Very well'. What, I
asked him, has become of the old virtues of the 'quality
press' of decades gone by, when a person might say he
was near-brought up on, or educated by, *The Times* and
Guardian? 'You can still find those virtues in some newspapers, but not in any national newspapers. You will find
them in the local press, the *Yorkshire Post* for instance.'
Do you read the *Yorkshire Post*? 'I don't, but I sense it.
Or in the *Glasgow Herald*, which I was reading all week
at the Edinburgh Festival. You will find such virtues there.'

In the 1950s, many in the educated middle class – my
father, for instance – would read the *Sunday Times* and
the *Observer* from cover to cover, almost as if their
intellectual lives depended upon them. 'I still read them,'
said G. gloomily. What virtues do you feel that present-
day quality newspapers lack? 'They lack several things.
One is caution. It is clear that they often print the first
thing that comes into their editors' heads and which they
think will attract readers. They also increasingly lack
literacy. The main elements both of the quality and the
tabloid press, starting with most of the editors, are no

longer fully literate. They do not read; many are illiterate.'
They cannot really be 'illiterate', said I. Do you not mean
semi-literate? 'Illiterate in journalistic terms.' Meaning
what? 'Incapable of identifying good writing, and being
unconcerned that they cannot identify it.'

Does it matter *sub specie aeternitatis*? I asked. 'One is
not entitled to view things from an eternal viewpoint,'
answered G. in his familiar wry fashion. 'If they are bad
today, that is all that should concern us. If they are to be
good tomorrow that is no great consolation.' But does
it really matter any longer that so much of the press,
including the 'quality' newspapers – particularly *The
Times*, the *Sunday Times* and the *Observer* – are as bad
as they are today? 'It matters because they still exercise an
enormous influence, and for the most part it is exercised
for the bad. I can barely recall a case in the recent period
when a good or valuable cause was being supported by
the press.'

What causes ought the press to be espousing which it
does not? 'It does not in a genuine fashion espouse the
cause of the arts, the cause of education, or truly virtuous
political causes. It espouses all the wrong causes, or does
not espouse anything at all. That is the kindest comment I
can make.' But the press is full of criticism of the education
system, for instance. 'Yes, but primarily in order to make
a sensation of educational difficulties, and to frighten its
readers. The press does not advocate any constructive
solutions. But that is also true of the political parties which
are completely lost where education is concerned.'

I still do not grasp what a 'genuine' espousal of good
causes by the press would be, said I. 'A genuine espousal
is one characterised by a feeling of real moral conviction.
Newspapers rarely persuade me that they possess it. You
feel that almost every newspaper is circumscribed by prior

considerations of circulation. It is unusual for a newspaper to conduct a campaign which would put its circulation at risk. It would be surprising if it did,' G. added. 'A newspaper is a purely commercial undertaking animated by no lofty motives. My assertion would be disputed by some of the newspapers themselves, but no perceptive person would dissent from it, even if the mass of a particular newspaper's ignorant readership might believe otherwise.'

You are surely conflating the 'quality press' and the 'tabloids' in these judgments, I said. Or are you implying that the distinctions between them are narrowing? 'They are certainly narrowing. There is not all that much ethical distinction between them. Such distinction as there is is more a class distinction, and points rather to distinctions of education among their various readerships. Large numbers of people are not educated enough to take any newspaper,' G. declared. 'The idea of spreading a newspaper across the breakfast table – avoiding the coffee pot – and reading out passages to other members of the family is a totally middle-class conception. If so-called quality newspapers – *The Times*, the *Telegraph*, the *Observer*, the *Guardian* – have any remaining educative influence, it is an influence which is exaggerated in the newspapers' own estimations, and is confined to the middle classes.'

You do not mention the *Independent* in your list of 'quality' newspapers, said I. 'It is arguable whether it should be included.' Why should it not be? 'The *Independent* has such financial problems that it cannot afford to be beyond suspicion as to whether it has convictions at all. On the whole, and in regard to its problems, it could at most be said to have been quite courageous in relation to the Royal Family, towards which it originally swore a Trappist vow of silence. But it has subsequently changed its position, because it realises that royalty represents a topic of very great public interest. If a newspaper does not attempt to satisfy such interest, it is deliberately abstaining from providing the public with what most of the public feels it should have.' Should it have it? I asked. 'It is perfectly entitled to news and comment about royalty, provided that the comment is not servile and the news too frequent or destructive,' G. answered.

In all such criticisms of the press, quality or tabloid, what virtues are we looking for? 'We are looking for an unqualified approval of one or more causes which are rightly regarded as virtues. There is an enormous range of possibilities and they are easily identified, including support for the NSPCC and the Salvation Army,' said G. with heavy irony.

Yes, but given the pressures of the market, surely such expectation that the press will adopt 'virtuous causes' is wholly unrealistic? 'It is unrealistic to expect a newspaper to adopt causes which have a real and detrimental effect upon its finances. A newspaper which was strident in its support of the anti-smoking lobby or in espousing teetotalism would do itself financial harm; the advocacy of a life without alcohol would not only lose a large number of readers but offend the brewers. It would cause some difficulty within the newspaper itself,' said G. with a chuckle. You want virtue from the press while knowing how difficult it is for them to pursue it? 'All worthy causes are easy to advocate but hard to pursue,' said G. Isn't the expectation itself pie-in-the-sky? 'Not quite pie-in-the-sky. Every so often a newspaper will come out with a leader condemning some popular practice on ethical grounds. But this is a very rare occurrence, whose frequency is also limited by political factors. Most newspapers subscribe to a political position. Virtue is generally not part of a political programme.'

Then most of what you hope for in the way of the espousal of good causes cannot be expected? 'It could be expected,' G. replied trenchantly, 'if the cause had a sufficiently valuable public aspect. It is also right to expect a newspaper to submit to some unpopularity as the price of espousing certain virtuous causes. But it is very rare, particularly in the case of national newspapers. They could do it, but they won't do it. Almost every virtuous cause – the condemnation of the bad side of wealth, for example – is bad for newspapers. I am an avid reader of them, but I do not recall any such attack on wealth.' You might see it in *Socialist Worker*, said I. 'That may be,' G. replied, 'but I do not regard *Socialist Worker* as a newspaper. The so-called "quality" press is too anxious not to court unpopularity with its readers, even when there is no great danger of it. It has proved particularly difficult for newspapers to take a genuine and sustained stand for decency when popular opinion is against them.'

For example? 'Take the recent refusal of a posthumous pardon for the boy Bentley. Most perceptive people would think it horribly wrong to have hanged a nineteen-year-old with a history of mental inadequacy for a crime of murder, in which he had had no substantial part except for the uttering of the questionable phrase "Let him have it!", and which could have been an instruction to his partner to surrender the gun the latter was holding. Bentley then kept himself under arrest, without restraint and without running away. Any sensible body of people, upon considering all the evidence without passion, would now, I believe, reject the possibility of Bentley's guilt.'

What has this to do with a virtuous press? said I. 'If there had been at the time, or was now, a powerful press advocacy for a pardon, there would have been a greater chance of gaining it. It is, of course, an hypocritical, or at least impractical, thing to pardon a man who has already been hanged,' G. continued. 'But it would give us the feeling that we were not guilty of the enormity which was committed against him decades ago. The Home Secretary's recent response [to refuse a pardon] was craven.' Why, do you think, did he not grant it? 'Because he felt an overriding duty to maintain the establishment in the positions it had taken. It was the establishment which allowed this boy to be hanged without permitting the jury's recommendation of mercy to be passed to the Home Secretary of the day, Sir Maxwell Fyfe, who was himself a man as near inhuman as anyone could imagine. The judge had determined that someone should hang for the murder of a policeman. For him, the hanging of an innocent man represented an advance towards a more civilised society. And since there are always fewer sensible people than idiotic people, and a press unwilling to espouse virtuous causes, he could rely on mass approval for his judgment.'

Do the 1950s and 1960s, to go back no further, nevertheless seem like halcyon days to you in the history of the press? 'I do not know about halcyon days, but newspapers were not then selecting individuals for destruction by whim, nor were they set upon the demolition of a valuable British institution such as the monarchy.' Did you too, in that period, read the *Sunday Times* and *Observer* as a source of instruction? 'I read both of them with respect in that period, and I am sure I was influenced by their views and opinions.' Do you now approach even some of the quality press with anticipatory distaste? 'It varies from paper to paper. Of the Sunday papers, I think that the *Sunday Telegraph* is the best. Its political position is clear-cut, its opinions are often written to be obnoxious,

but this is better than the confused positions of a newspaper like the *Observer*.'

From what do you think these problems – of 'illiteracy',
destructiveness, political confusion and so on – derive?
'All this,' G. answered, 'is attributable to the proprietors'
choice of unsuitable editors. If you have editors who can
hardly read, you are unlikely to win literary prizes for
your newspapers.' But the causes surely go deeper than
the poor choice of personnel? 'It is due also to the
increasing lack of education in the reading public. They
have become less selective. You and I,' G. continued,
'would find it strange to believe that there are such large
numbers of people who deliberately choose to read the
Sun, the *People*, or the *Sunday Mirror*. To us, supposedly
educated men, these are impossible and ridiculous
choices.'

But in the 1950s there were also newspapers like the
Sunday Pictorial. 'We did not choose to read them,' G.
said briefly. No, said I, and we do not read the *Sun* either.
My point is that the tabloid press and the low quality
of its editors are not new phenomena. 'They come much
more to our notice than they did, their influence is larger,
and they run campaigns which have nothing genuinely to
do with moral causes and which increasingly displease us.'
The fact that their reach is wider afflicts us more because
it has a more general impact on the culture? 'Certainly,'
said G.

Do you agree that newspapers ought to be better than
they are, but that every kind of obstacle – financial,
educational, personal, together with diverse failures of will
– stands in their way? 'Whether they *ought* to be better
than they are is a difficult matter to determine,' replied G.
sardonically. 'But that they cannot be better than they are
without a negative effect on their finances is something

they accept before I do. A newspaper quickly learns that if it does not wish to antagonise its readership a certain kind of moral assertion is better avoided. Moreover, the press conforms to the prevailing opinion in relation to most moral issues, or will in general avoid them if they are serious matters of contention. I do not know of any newspaper which would campaign for or against abortion. It might be that the *Tablet* does, but that is not a newspaper.'

Do you mean that you would like to open your *Observer* and find in it campaigning articles or editorials on the issue of abortion? 'I would not subject the logic of my argument to the test of practicality,' said G. with a laugh. 'But newspapers will not espouse serious moral causes, and certainly not for long, upon which their readerships would be divided. They only espouse causes which they know their readerships would support, and then delude themselves with the belief that they have given their readers a moral lead in those matters.'

Surely, all this merely shows again how hard it is for newspapers to pursue the virtues which you recommend? 'It is hard,' said G. 'But they could take much greater risks than they do of adopting positions which are not consonant with popular approval.' But if to cure such matters were to lead newspapers to lose even more readers than most of them are already doing, I persisted, how can proprietors and their editors be blamed for their present sins of omission and commission? Isn't this the heart of the dilemma? 'It is agreeable to think that on many crucial matters the newspapers do not exercise an evil influence,' G. replied, changing direction. 'It is rare, for example, to find an attack on organised religion. Such an attack would itself have a damaging circulation effect.' It does not stop increasingly sly remarks about the Jews, said I. 'That is a different question. It is rare to find an open attack on the Jews. One can say that anti-semitism is not a feature of the British press.' Perhaps, but it did not stop the *Sunday Times* from hiring David Irving. 'That was an isolated incident. Moreover, I think the *Sunday Times* now regrets it. But if you employ an editor who is totally incapable of making a moral judgment, as I rate the editor of the *Sunday Times* to be incapable, you must expect some startling support, or condemnation, of particular causes.'

Yet, given the pressures, is it the fault of an editor like Andrew Neil that he is driven to the vulgarities he commits? 'I think it is. The editor determines, and is responsible for, everything that goes in his paper.' He also has to please his proprietor, said I. 'In certain respects the editor enjoys a large area of independence. Indeed, what is bad for a newspaper is the impression, as in the case of the *Observer*, that its editor's opinions are subservient to those of its proprietor.' Nevertheless, once the readers of the tabloids or of a newspaper like the *Sunday Times* have become habituated to a regular diet of vulgarity and crassness, do not their expectations themselves become a constraint upon any change of direction?

'There is abundant evidence that the readerships of the tabloids in particular have little resistance to vulgarity and to other matters which, if reformed, would make their papers better. Moreover, the readerships of the so-called "quality" press also bring little support to the advocacy of moral causes by the papers they read. In consequence, even a newspaper like the *Sunday Times* no longer has an identifiable moral quality of any kind.'

Perhaps these distastes of yours about the press, which I share, are merely a symptom of the ageing process, said I. Have not the middle-aged and old always exclaimed, 'O tempora! O mores!'?' 'I do not think my criticisms are a symptom of age,' G. replied. 'As soon as I was capable of rational thought I formed certain views, and had certain criteria for holding them, which have remained unchanged. You do not suffer a sudden declension in your judgment merely because you are older than you were.' But after the age of 50, does not everything tend to seem worse than it was? 'Such generalisations are very unsafe. Educated men would not suddenly think that things had got worse just because they were a year or two older than they had been.

'There is no doubt that newspapers are worse. They are less responsible, less controlled, less measured, less literate, and in many other ways less acceptable, in particular in the way they attack individuals and seek to ruin them.' Did it arouse your tender-heartedness even towards a David Mellor? 'My reaction to Mr Mellor,' said G., 'was inspired by his solicitude towards the PLO. This showed a want of judgment. I was not, however, concerned for his extra-marital activities.' Does this mean that you forgave him all his trespasses, except his position on the Palestinian issue? 'I would have been prepared to forgive him many things, but not his damaging concern, or alleged concern, for the arts. He represented everything against which I campaigned in my opposition to a Ministry for the Arts.' But you made an exception for Jennie Lee, said I. 'Because she had a genuine belief that the arts are good for people.' Did not Mellor believe that too? 'I do not know what he believed. But whatever it was, he did not seek to achieve it. If there is to be such a thing as a Minister for the Arts it ought to be anyone but a David Mellor.'

To go back to the press, is there nothing to be done? 'One should not despair, or consider that virtue will never win. But it is very far behind vice, and shows no sign of catching up on it.' Could one not say that the decline in quality of a newspaper like *The Times* is nevertheless an overestimated matter? 'Insofar as any valuable institution enters into decline it matters. We are a better informed, responsible society if we have newspapers which will address themselves to real issues in educated language. The disappearance of these qualities from any great newspaper is a national tragedy.' Have they disappeared from *The Times*? 'Their disappearance from *The Times* has been quite considerable.' Who suffers? 'The British people.' What are they losing? 'They are losing the opportunity of understanding important things which are explained to them with lucidity and intelligence.'

Would it be going too far to say that the press has been 'corrupted' or that it is actually 'corrupt'? 'Some sections of the press are thoroughly corrupt. "Cheque-book journalism" is just another term for corruption. The belief that you can buy everybody you want if you are sufficiently rich as a newspaper is a very dangerous belief in a civilised society.'

But as well as failing, as you would see it, to espouse the right causes, what are the wrong causes which the newspapers espouse? 'That is to some extent a matter of political opinion,' G. replied. 'I would regard it as a wrong cause to espouse Conservative policy,' he said, levity returning briefly. 'Many would disagree with me, but such is my tolerance I am happy to let them remain alive,' he added.

All these moral objections to the press surely point only in the direction of censorship, for how else could they be cured? 'A newspaper can advocate a moral policy without it being enforced anywhere else.' said G. 'Take pornography. Occasionally, a newspaper casts a side-glance of disapproval at it, but that does not imply censorship. Censorship is a menace to newspapers.' But without it, or without some form of licensing, how can the Augean stables of the tabloids be cleaned out? 'By my favourite recipe, by having proprietors with a strong moral sense.' But, surely, said I, most newspapers get proprietors, as well as editors, in the same way as they acquire readers – according to the law of the jungle. 'The inducement to own a newspaper derives, first of all, from the influence and power it gives. Secondly, it is regarded as a profitable investment. Thirdly, it is held to be intrinsically interesting to own a newspaper.'

Nevertheless, whatever the varied attractions of owning a newspaper, how can a proprietor, even supposing him possessed of the virtues you or I might desire, sustain indefinitely the competitive position of his newspaper without compromise of standards? 'It is certainly true that the competitive situation leads most newspapers to lower their standards. How low is sometimes a matter of chance, but it is increasingly disgracefully low. At its lowest it is characterised by victimisation, invasion of privacy, and cheque-book bribery. At the same time, the attitude to invasion of privacy, for instance, is that restraint on the press is bad for newspapers.'

What would you actually estimate the purpose of the British tabloid press to be? 'Its purpose is to sell the largest number of newspapers, by whatever means are available and at the largest profit possible. That is how it justifies itself to itself. It is not a justification many of us would wish to share.' No, but could it not be said that a good deal of snobbishness enters into objections to a newspaper like the *Sun*? 'You and I are people who have on the whole been brought up in an atmosphere of relative decency. We have been educated to a rather different level from that of the average reader of the *Sun* and *News of the World*. It is not surprising that some of the things they do are not congenial. But that is not in itself ground for changing them. To get better newspapers one must hope for better educated readerships. In this country,' G. added, 'such is the standard of education, that hope must be forlorn.' A dismal outlook, said I. 'The outlook for a better educated people exerting a better educated influence must be doubtful,' said G. Then can we not try to find virtue in the energy, style, or even perverse attractiveness of the tabloids? 'The devil has all the best tunes,' G. replied. 'That is true in all matters.'

Nevertheless, could it not be said that the tabloids speak in some useful fashion for the 'common man'? 'Like the "man on the Clapham omnibus", he is a fiction. One of the worst features of the claim of the tabloid press to "speak for the common man" is that they insert into his mouth, or voice, their own odious opinions.' But was not the headline 'Gotcha!', referring to the sinking of the *Belgrano* in the Falklands War, *vox populi*? 'I do not think there was great popular enthusiasm for the Falklands War, certainly at its outset. Such "popularity" as it acquired was the result of skilfully-managed propaganda by Mrs Thatcher; she could not have continued her triumphalist cause without newspaper support. I regret that I lacked the courage to speak in opposition to the Falklands War during the House of Lords debate on the matter. In the speeches made in the morning of the debate there was such unanimity in favour of the war that I feared that everyone would fall on me if I spoke against it. I found myself conveniently engaged in the afternoon of the debate at an arts engagement. It suited my moral cowardice very well' – this said with a chuckle – 'and acquitted me of the necessity of returning to make what would have been a thoroughly unpopular speech.'

You say it would not have been popular to oppose the

war, yet you maintain at the same time that the tabloid press is not vox pop. 'It is not vox pop. It believes that it is. In fact, the vox pop which it projects, or attempts to project, is its own voice, not the voice of the people.' How can you be so sure? I asked. 'I can entertain a sensible suspicion of it.' But it *becomes* vox pop, does it not? 'That is the vice. People are influenced by these rubbishy papers to adopt their rubbishy views.' The populace itself is innocent? 'Innocent,' said G., 'is too exonerating a word. It is not guilty in the sense that, when left to itself, the noises which it makes are not the noises of the popular press.'

Whose noises is the popular press emitting? 'Its own noises,' replied G. 'Sometimes they are the noises of the proprietor, sometimes of the editor, sometimes of the people who at any given time have influence over the editor.' The editors of the tabloids, then, are not speaking for anything which might be termed 'national' or 'public' opinion? 'They are speaking for their own generally reactionary opinions, or, if obsequious, echoing the sounds which their proprietors would like to hear.'

Why do you suppose that the British tabloid press is, by common consent, worse than any other nation's? 'I do not know the financial structure of the press of other countries. But one must conclude that the British press is owned by less responsible proprietors.' A German newspaper like *Bild Zeitung* is crass, too, but I fancy 'Gotcha!' has no equals, said I. 'There is an inherent vulgarity in that which cannot be found anywhere else. For a mass circulation newspaper to demonstrate such vulgarity is not a good thing for society.' But are not 'vulgarity' and 'mass circulation' synonyms? 'If they are synonyms,' G. replied, 'they ought not to be so. If they are, these papers are doing nothing but harm.'

153

But if something serious has been happening to the education system, as you and I believe, is it not bound to be reflected in the culture of which the tabloid press is a part? 'We have to recognise that our educational standards, by the side of other countries, are low and do not get better. In particular, the education of the working class – to use a snobbish phrase – is of lower quality than it used to be, and the worst in Western Europe.' Is there, then, not a closer congruence than you care to admit between what the tabloids say and what their readers want them to say, and the ways in which they say it? 'The tabloid newspapers do not know what their readers want them to say,' G. insisted. 'They cannot know. They can only guess. And a guess from a vulgar mind will be a vulgar guess.'

No doubt, but the 'guesses' of the tabloid press may not be so aberrant as one would like to believe. 'What you are saying is that the tabloid newspapers have recognised that the state of society is low, and see it as their duty to pander to it.' It might be true, said I. 'In which case,' said G., 'it is a disaster. You and I must toil against it. Our lives are dedicated to the contrary proposition.'

Has tycoon ownership not played a large part in debasing the standards of the press, the quality press included? 'Yes. Tycoon ownership is an entirely undiscriminating ownership. Bearing in mind that it is the quality of the owner which determines the quality of the editor, who in turn determines the quality of the journalists, the consequence is that the choice of editors and journalists is in many cases vulgar and undiscriminating.' ('The Astors were more civilised people than any of today's tycoons,' G. added.) But if you go back a decade or two, Roy Thomson was hardly a man of great culture, was he? 'He was not a man of great culture. But newspaper-owners like him, although they had a simple preoccupation with profit, did not debase their newspapers to any great extent in the pursuit of it. Nor do I think they would have appointed editors and journalists of the low quality that are now to be found in certain national newspapers. They will go to lengths in pursuit of profit which would not have been possible earlier, particularly in the victimisation of individuals.'

Newspapers and their editors, including some of the broadsheets, may be becoming ever coarser, but how is it that such a large proportion of proprietors are notably coarser also? 'They are coarser because restraints have disappeared. Newspapers have been permitted to be sold to entirely unsuitable people. If you examine the ideologies of the owners, Murdoch is not really interested in newspapers at all. He is interested only in the profit which he derives from them, but he has no sense of responsibility. He seems to be motivated in Britain by one ambition: to destroy the Royal Family. It is not a kindly ambition, nor to the benefit of the country. In other respects, he might be a model proprietor.

'Harmsworth,' continued G., 'is a more neutral character. He runs his newspapers in accordance with a very simple formula: he would be devastated if he lost Nigel Dempster, a man about whose policy and veracity we should all have some doubts. Stevens is a different kettle of fish. He came into the newspaper world from accountancy, and remains exclusively interested in accountancy. The only ownerships in which one might place some hope are those of the *Guardian* and, perhaps, the *Independent*.'

Would you say that, in addition to the matters we have discussed, the influence of the press is diminishing in the face of television? 'It is still influential not only because it lasts,' G. replied, 'but because written judgments are generally more persuasive. It was only when newspapers became tepid towards Mrs Thatcher that it was possible for her colleagues to remove her. Television is a more ephemeral propaganda. A newspaper is there to be kept. Newspapers, however, do not have the insidious effect of television on the young. A child might say, "Please, daddy, can I stay up to watch television?", but no child would say, "Please, daddy, may I stay up to read *The Times*?" ' (At this sally, G.'s merriment was unconfined.) They might sit up reading the *Sun*, said I. 'That is another matter,' G. declared, 'but even that is unlikely, or that they would sit up to read anything whatever. It would be a blessing,' G. added, 'were they to evince a desire to read at all. A child is better exposed to any kind of written words than to television, except those which deliberately set out to corrupt him.'

Nevertheless, there have been many instances of television documentaries taking up the moral issues of the day – of hunger in Africa, of corruption in local government, of miscarriages of justice and so forth – which show up the weaknesses of the press in precisely the ways of which you complain. 'That is true. Television and radio are better on moral issues than are newspapers.' Why should this be? I asked. 'Because the ownership of the major television and radio organisations is now more diversified than that of the national press. A television company will generally be owned by quite a large number of people, with a diversity of shareholders, and therefore susceptible to pressures which in many instances might not be regarded as unvirtuous. They are also, by and large, more in touch with the feeling of the day and the varieties of culture. Particularly,' G. added, 'in relation to the admiration for pop singers.' But isn't that precisely what produces the vulgarities of which you were complaining? 'Of course it is. It also produces diversity of opinion and the taking up of moral causes which you do not find in newspapers.'

But what kind of truth is it that we get from television? 'We have invited this very powerful medium into our sitting rooms, a medium that, despite the impact of written judgments on educated people, can have a much more pervasive influence than the one that is kept outside the door.' Don't you think that one of the effects of television has been to drive the press into trying to match the visual sensations it offers? 'I think that in this respect it has had a debasing effect on the newspapers. But it is more noteworthy that there have not been any significant writers or thinkers produced by television. Here is an all-pervading medium which has produced no one individual of intellectual distinction.' Perhaps, said I; but it has produced informed popularisers of useful knowledge like David Attenborough, or, earlier, Jacob Bronowski. 'They are not names which resound through the world,' said G., without expression.

Is this lack a fault of the medium as such? 'Not necessarily. It is not in itself a defect that the medium has to appeal to a mass audience.' Does it have to? 'Of course it does.' Why? 'It has to pay.' And hence becomes degraded? 'It does not have to be a degraded appeal. Unfortunately, today, notwithstanding television's other virtues, a large extent of the appeal is degraded.' Why? 'Because the programme-makers have in general come to believe that programmes should appeal to the ignorant. The quality of many of the media controllers – the people controlling the programmes – is terrifying. When I attended the Edinburgh Festival the other week, my hotel was invaded by a gathering of them. I do not think that ordinary journalists would have aroused my critical instincts as much as these people. They were brash, noisy, ignorant, socially uneducated and vulgar.' Nothing else? 'Nothing.' Is it in the nature of the medium itself, I asked again, or the technology, or what?

'For obvious commercial reasons television has to appeal to vast numbers. The ignorant people in charge of it believe that it must therefore have the lowest possible standards.' Despite the fact that television intermittently does well by moral causes? 'Despite the fact that there are very creditable personalities in television today who stand for positions which are morally right. But they are few in number.'

If all this is so, said I, is it a reason for the BBC to follow suit? 'The BBC follows suit because over the years it has succumbed to the unfortunate doctrine that it has to be "competitive" with the commercial television companies. You and I well know that if the standards of Reith are to be maintained the BBC cannot compete with ITV. The very attempt is to lower its standards.'

But, as in the case of the tabloid press, is not the mass television medium bound almost by definition to dissolve such standards? 'Not necessarily,' said G. 'You can start with potato crisps as an example. They too require a mass market but that does not require low standards. In fact, potato crisps have improved with the years.' Potato crisps are not television programmes, said I. 'That is true,' G. declared. 'But the problem of the mass media is not ultimately to be found either in their audiences, however badly educated, or in the nature of the media themselves, but in those who are in charge of them. Anything which is designed by vulgar programme-makers to have a spurious or debased appeal to a vast quantity of people is bound to lower its standards.'

And this is at the heart of the moral conundrum, said I:

it is impossible to raise those standards if to do so is to forfeit the readerships, audiences and revenues which the media are seeking. 'Absolute good is impossible in any human institution. The only issue is how far it departs from the absolute. Sometimes, it will be a very considerable distance. Galsworthy, a very great moralist, took the view that mass taste is a brutal taste. But we came to accept that the influence of the old Hollywood films was not wholly disastrous, because the people who made them recognised that, in order to have a mass appeal, the films also could not disgust or alienate the mind. Although they were often rubbish, they were not wicked rubbish. Hollywood people imposed their own discipline, including a code under which it was not possible to have villainy triumph.'

Now, said I, Indian villagers are being subjected by Rupert Murdoch to American game-shows by satellite transmission, at all hours of the day and night. 'Most Indian villagers will be protected from them by their ignorance of English and by Rupert Murdoch's ignorance of Hindi.' But the visual image requires no language, I rejoined. 'True,' said G., 'it could all be done in dumb-show, but the producers would be likely to object.' Television pornography by satellite needs no commentary, said I. 'The least of the enormities is nakedness,' said G. 'We have all become habituated to it. It should not arouse any strong feelings.' Does it not in you? 'I always used to say that after I had passed seventy I would shed any carnal impulse. It might have been too hopeful,' he added. Was it? 'I do not think it was.'

[10]

Some Observations on Women

Would you think, I asked G., that after the matters we have discussed most recently, the subject of women was a light or a serious subject? 'I do not think it is a light subject. Indeed, when a bachelor speaks about women it must create the suspicion that he has been born with a prejudice against them.' Why do you have such a prejudice? 'I have no prejudice against them. I accept them as constituting approximately half of the human race, and I entertain no more hostility to them than I do to the human race as a whole.' And how much hostility is that? I asked. 'On the whole, I like human beings well enough,' G. replied.

But is there anything about women that you dislike which you do not find, or do not dislike, in men? 'There are certain attributes in women which are less likeable than similar attributes found in the male.' What do you have in mind? 'They are obviously more conscious of their own status than men,' answered G. Are they? 'It is built-in,' said G. flatly. 'They have a built-in sense of inferiority for being women. In consequence, they are much more on the defensive than men about their status and position, and about the justification for their own existence.' Do they need to justify it? 'They do not need, just as men do not need, to justify their existence.' What evidence is there for what you say about women's defensiveness? 'If you know a woman for any length of time,' G. replied, 'you are bound to detect some form of self-justificatory attitude about their existence.'

And you actively dislike women for this? 'They are less likeable for it.' Feminists, said I, would not regard you with much approval for that; you are hardly an exemplar of the 'New Man'. 'No, I am not,' G. cheerfully declared. You also said that women's 'consciousness of their own status' was 'less likeable' than when the same thing was found in men. Why should it not be equally dislikeable in men? 'Because there is less of it, and in women it is almost a reflex reaction. There are many men who suffer from excessive self-importance, which is a form of consciousness of status, but it is not so disagreeable because it is not so aggressive. Moreover, it does not derive in men from consciousness of difference of sex.' It is this consciousness which in women gives their defensiveness a dislikeable edge, for you? 'Yes, that is true. Assertions which are based on sex status are not wholly likeable.'

What kind of assertions are you thinking of? I asked. 'Above all, assertions by women about their role and their value. On the whole, men are wise not to challenge women as to their value,' G. added warily. Yet, if you are right, women plainly believe themselves to be challenged by men in this respect, or they would not be so 'defensive'? 'Yes. They believe in general that the majority of men hold them to be in an inferior position, and, often, that they need to challenge this at the earliest possible time. This can cause difficult situations,' G. murmured.

It sounds to me, said I, that you are more easily irritated by, and more quickly become impatient with, women than men. 'Yes,' said G., 'I think I do. It is probably a fault, but I think it is true. However, I also have a possibly excessive consciousness of their rare qualities, based on the experience of several women who have served me over the years.' Nevertheless, said I, I am still interested to know why women irritate you more than do men. 'It is because I am conscious of the fact that in any argument with them on the question of their value and status you are unlikely to succeed.' Do you mean that you feel overcome by, and therefore irritated by, women's defensive arguments? 'If you are confronted with an essentially female argument, you have no equipment with which to deal with it. An essentially masculine argument you can understand to the very roots.'

So you feel generally disarmed of your capacities in contention with a woman? 'I am convinced of the futility of trying to persuade a woman not to be a woman,' said G. Have you known many scolds and harridans who were to be avoided at all costs? 'I have known many human beings whom one had to avoid at all costs,' G. answered. 'The categories you mention are not confined to women, nor are women more largely represented in them than men. But the attributes women bring to discussion include not only persistence in argument, but persistence in fallacious argument. Men will dry up sooner, and not persist with unattainable or impossible assertion. Women think that to give in is a reflection on their sex.'

If this is one of the effects of women doubting their value and status is there not something tragic about it? 'There is something tragic about women,' G. replied. 'They obviously get the rough end of the social stick. If you examine the situation in detail, and although women will hotly dispute what I am about to assert, a woman's life is a life which generally depends upon a marriage, successful or not. There is no doubt that an unmarried woman in most cases regards herself as a failure, even though women will resent the suggestion. An unmarried woman who does not regard herself as a failure for being unmarried is to be counted successful for that reason alone,' G. added wryly.

All this implies that women have made no social 'progress' at all, said I. 'There is a belief, which men seek to cultivate, that the status of women has greatly improved in recent times. If you examine this belief closely, it is not a fact. Although ostensibly men may profess to regard and treat women on equal terms, it is more a pretence than a reality.'

Do you yourself regard and treat women as equal? I asked. 'No,' said G., 'I have a deep-seated conviction that women are intellectually inferior to men. It is probably an unfair conviction, but it is there.' But that is precisely the male attitude which helps to induce in women the 'defensiveness' of which you were just complaining, said I. 'The fact that *I* believe they are inferior intellectually does not mean that *they* believe they are inferior, even if their defensiveness may reveal that they have a sense of it. Indeed, it is unlikely that I could convince any being, whether a woman or a dog, that it was intellectually inferior. It would be a hopeless task; neither would believe it, nor want to believe it. Moreover, vanity, which is a characteristic of all human beings but of women in particular, prevents them acknowledging the fact.'

Where did you get this conviction about the intellectual inferiority of women? 'It is not possible to say where I got it. But it is not as if I came up against evidence of it which left me with a sudden sense of shock. It was probably born with me.' Yet you said at the outset that you had no prejudice against women. 'What was born with me was the capacity to recognise facts; a prejudice is an unwillingness to face facts. Since, from the moment of birth, there stares at you the fact that women are in general intellectually inferior to men, it is not a prejudice to believe that fact.' Nevertheless, is it not a hard thing for any woman to hear such an opinion from a man? 'If you start from the belief which I hold about them, and are thinking to yourself "this is an inferior mind speaking", women are in difficulties when they open their mouths. I admit that it might be an unfair basis on which to judge them.'

It is not so much an unfair as a very harsh judgment, said I. 'Any judgment which is instinctive may have some appearance of harshness,' G. declared. 'If you have believed all your life that a woman with a long nose is ugly, this is a harsh judgment' (laughing), 'and brutally affects every long-nosed woman.' But there are many intelligent and educated, as well as short-nosed, women, I said. 'If you find men with humps disagreeable, it is obviously idiotic to suppose that every man has a hump,' was G.'s oblique reply.

Some of your women friends will be disgruntled to hear these opinions. 'I do not think they will be surprised if they know me,' said G. phlegmatically. But don't you think your views unfair? 'Nothing in my views is intended to be unfair to women. My powers of observation may be faulty, but this is what I see. Obviously different men see women differently. There is little doubt,' G. added, 'that Abélard would have regarded Héloise with great admiration, affection and love even after he had been castrated.'

Nevertheless, your suggestion that, in general, men who claim to regard women equally do not do so means that women are tragically deceived by such pretences. 'It is tragic,' G. declared, 'in relation to women's real social situation. Even today the goal of most women has to be a successful marriage, or, as the case may be, a successful liaison.'

But if a man's status, as in your case, is not devalued by being unmarried, surely men, and especially bachelors, ought in fairness to object to this devaluation when it is suffered by women? 'It is certainly true that men are not devalued in this way. They might be considered eccentric, or as worshipping false idols, but I do not think any man is looked down upon for not marrying. He may even be looked up to with envy and wonder as to how he had contrived the happy situation.'

But to say so, I protested, itself disparages or devalues women, as does declaring them to be intellectually inferior. 'I think that remarks which derive from genuine and honest observation are not open to criticism. You cannot criticise the making of a remark if it is honest. Nor does what I say discount the amazing virtues of women, including their courage and caring. If one has an ailment it would be a very foolish person who sent for a man, although men are also capable of being caring nurses. In fact, caring is a quality of which women have a monopoly, because they do it unreasonably.' What do you mean? 'They do it without judgment, because they are quicker to sense the need for it.'

Despite this kind of praise, women are bound to have a hard time of it if even humane individuals think as you do of the female intellect. 'I am sufficiently sad and modest,' G. replied, 'to think that my views do not influence the whole of mankind, or womankind. Nearly all the things I have said to you are gut responses, and may have less validity than more considered reactions.'

Is it not men's duty to help women fight for their rights? 'I think it is. Or, more accurately, it is men's duty not to stand in their path. At this moment, for instance, the rewards given to women for their labour are something less than the rewards given to men for the same or similar work. That cannot be right.' But how has it come about? 'It has grown up in a process of discrimination which is centuries old.' That is hardly surprising, seeing that you too think women intellectually inferior by nature, said I. 'It *is* surprising, since the inequality to which I was pointing relates largely to activities where intellect is not an essential requirement. A window-cleaner, male or female, does not need to be a senior wrangler,' said G. jovially, 'just as a stoker needs only to distinguish between different kinds of coal.'

What do you think of feminism? I asked. 'If there wasn't a feminist argument, it would have to be invented,' G. replied. 'Women themselves by and large dislike too active feminists. Nevertheless, they need them. The causes in which women have succeeded, such as that led by Mrs Pankhurst for women's suffrage, were only gained by the involvement of individual women few in number and rare in their tribe. Florence Nightingale did more for her gender than she did for nursing. She was prepared to antagonise very influential males who wanted to snuff out the candle she was carrying.'

You might have wanted to do the same at the time, said I. 'It is possible, but very unlikely. I would never have joined any cause which was opposed to the interests of the great majority of mankind, or which was not supported by invincible reason. I am always prepared to enlist on the side of the oppressed – largely because it is easy to justify my moral concern,' said G., with ironic self-deprecation.

Do you not think that men in general ought to be enlisting alongside women in the struggle for greater 'women's rights'? 'This is a cause which has few attractions for a man, although I can see considerable merit in it,' G. answered. You wouldn't go to the barricades in the feminist cause? 'I would not go to the barricades for any woman's cause. As it is, women are sufficiently clamant to make it impossible for a man's voice to be heard above them.'

You declared earlier that a bachelor might be thought 'eccentric' or to be 'worshipping false idols' for not marrying. What kind of bachelor are you? 'There are indeed various types of bachelor, including the accidental bachelor, a category in which I would include myself. I am an accidental bachelor in the sense that I did not make a considered decision to remain a bachelor, even if all my instincts encouraged me to that.' Does this mean that you are really a constitutional bachelor, who cannot, if the truth be known, stick women in any shape or form? 'I am not one such,' G. replied. 'On the contrary, I have had many close women friends, and still have them. I also had opportunities to marry, but it always impressed me that marriage would interfere with my ordered life.'

Do women then represent to you the spirit of disorder? 'On the contrary. It is not women but marriage which represents it to me. There is no doubt that marriage consumes a great deal of time that could be spent in advancing one's career.' That sounds a particularly egoistic ground for having rejected it. 'Indeed. It sets too much value on oneself, which one should not do,' said G. If a wife would have interfered with your 'ordered life', have your various *châtelaines* not done so also? 'Anyone who has some direction of your behaviour – and this must extend to a responsible housekeeper – is bound to interfere in some way with your existence. Any housekeeper worth her salt will constitute a gross interference with your personal liberty. She will, for instance, insist that you rise from your bed before lunch and even dictate what you should eat. Such housekeepers not only try to interfere but regard it as their duty to save one from the disadvantageous consequences of one's own choices. I am so well trained to resist such interferences that they have very modest success with me.'

That may be all very well with your housekeepers, said I, but what kind of 'interferences' do you suffer at the hands of your close women-friends? 'I will concede to them,' answered G., 'in any matter which I regard as unimportant. On the question of holidays, for instance, I compromise in such a fashion that I nearly always go to the place I choose.' That, said I, is a trivial victory; how do you avoid domination by them? 'One must fight quite hard to avoid domination by women. The difficulty is that they regard such domination as an element of caring. The more they care, the more they irritate the objects of their care, unreasonable as such irritation may be.'

It again strikes me how prone you seem to be to such 'irritation', said I. 'We all flatter ourselves on our noble qualities,' G. declared. 'I would put patience high among my own qualities. (It is a quality which has been demonstrated by my attitude to the proceedings going on between us.) But what is at least as important as controlling impatience is to control the show of impatience.' That suggests that beneath the surface of your seeming equanimity there might sometimes lurk feelings of profound disturbance. ' "Profound disturbance" and "lurk" are an exaggeration of my feelings. I can control unseemly displays of behaviour. I do not want to attack people,' G. said with a laugh. 'I do not get up and pull the table-cloth off the table. All these things require a measure of self-restraint.'

Do you like women? I asked. 'I do not think a generalisation in those terms can be made. It is like asking "Do you like donkeys?" I do not have an unselective affection for donkeys, or even baboons,' G. declared, laughing. Are you, I asked, seriously lumping together women, donkeys and baboons? 'You cannot have an unselective affection for any group of creatures, whatever they might be,' G. replied, unabashed; 'it is idiotic to state that one "likes women", just like that.'

Some men can be heard stating so, said I. 'They say they do. What it means is that when it comes to declaring a preference for a companion, they say that they prefer a woman. That is like saying, when they are going to buy a dog, that they prefer a dachshund to a bloodhound.' It sounds as if you put women in some kind of bestiary with donkeys, baboons and breeds of canines, said I. 'No. The attributes of a donkey, including a very inadequate brain, are possessed by a great number of human beings, women and men.' ('I have not known a single donkey obtain admission to a university,' added G.)

Do you think that 'liking' women and being 'attracted' by them are different things? 'There is a difference,' G. replied, 'but if you like an individual woman it will also be because you are attracted to her, although not necess-arily for a sexual reason.' Have you yourself ever suffered emotional turmoil caused by a woman, which made you unhappy? 'I don't think I have,' G. cautiously replied. 'That would relate to passion, or to love. Then, the likelihood of a woman causing turmoil is higher.' Have you been through that turmoil? I asked. 'No, never. On the whole, my emotional sights are kept pretty low,' G. added. Out of self-protection, or what? 'You cannot determine in advance what will engender an emotional, or irrational, reaction, but in my case it has not occurred to any great extent.' Is that a weakness or a strength of character? G. paused; a rare pause. 'I think it is an *advantage* of character. Whether it is a strength or weakness I cannot say.'

If you are not attracted to women in a fashion which generates such emotion, how else are you attracted? 'It may sound a condescending statement, but it is quite possible to like a woman for her mind.' Even if women are 'intellectually inferior'? 'That assertion,' G. declared, 'does not mean that there is not an enormous disparity between the most and the least intelligent of women. The fact that a woman falls short of the most intelligent of men does not diminish the capacity of women to impress you. Indeed, to like a woman for her mind is both an interesting and agreeable experience. There are a few women whom I welcome when they arrive precisely because I know that there is going to be an entertaining exchange between us.'

But would you choose to engage in a philosophical discussion about justice or ethics, say, with a woman? 'No,' answered G.. 'This is probably the result of an unreasoning prejudice, but I would not choose to have a philosophical discussion on any subject with a woman. With a man, you can start talking philosophically and the worst that might happen is that you would find he was idiotic. With a woman, an interesting exchange of views on a philosophical subject is a highly unlikely prospect.' For what reason? 'I was not responsible for the creation of mankind, so I cannot give a reason,' said G., with faint irritation.

What it comes to is that, for you, a true 'marriage of minds' was not possible with a woman? 'Since I never entered into any sort of marriage, that excluded any "marriage of minds". I do not want to enter into a "marriage of minds" with anyone,' G. added, 'least of all with a woman.'

Are you saying that there is in women some constitutional or genetic defect which prevents them thinking or talking philosophically? 'Their intellectual qualities are such that certain forms of conversational exchange with them may be impossible, others may be difficult, and others interesting but differing in quality from those with men.' This sounds, said I, like an elaborate version of the male cliché that women are 'mere flibbertygibbets'. 'I find that conversations about trivialities are more attractive to women than they are to men,' G. replied, unrepentant.

But if, believing them to be intellectually inferior, you don't even try to talk to your women friends about Plato or Spinoza, is it not your prejudice which prevents them from displaying their intellectual qualities to you? 'If I had endeavoured to talk about Plato or Spinoza with most men,' G. merrily replied, 'their own lack of understanding would have been horrifying, and their resistance brutal.' Here G. began to laugh until his eyes watered. 'If at a dinner party you were to ask your male neighbour "What are your views about Plato and Spinoza?" he would promptly leave the table,' G. continued, still laughing. 'But women have a lower threshold of boredom even than men, largely because most of them have had to suffer husbands over the generations.'

What you are saying will nevertheless be found highly irritating to many women, to put it mildly, said I. 'That may be so,' replied G.. 'But it does not apply to all women. There are obviously women who are very clever, well-informed and well-educated. But here one must pause, because of the unlikelihood that a woman in general will be as well-educated as a man.' Why? 'Because over the years they have had an inferior education to that of men, and one dictated by men. It may be to do women an injustice – which I am willing to do – but women have in general not fought for education as have men.'

But what about the pioneering women, the women who struggled in the nineteenth century for adequate educational provision for girls, the women whose endeavours led to the founding of Oxbridge colleges for women, and so on? 'A pioneer,' G. briefly replied, 'is not a characteristic figure of any tribe. That is why he or she is a pioneer.'

Do you then believe women to be the 'weaker sex' *as such*? 'To talk of women as a "weaker sex" is clearly to describe them in a way which gives some satisfaction to the male. They are clearly weaker physically. There has never, for example, been a female heavyweight boxing champion of the world.' (This was said laughing.) There are female wrestlers, however, said I. 'But they are not in competition with men.' But some athletic Amazons do approach the condition of men, said I. 'The fact that you have to use such an exceptionally tendentious word as "Amazon" signifies that you regard them as abnormal,' G. declared. 'The truth is that men have very nearly a monopoly of athletic prowess.' Is it not complete? 'No. I discovered in the Army [where G. played hockey] that there was nothing more lethal to men than an ATS hockey team. No male shin was left unbruised. But, over all, athletic prowess is a monopoly of men.'

In your perception of women, do they not have real 'strengths' which compensate them for their 'weaknesses' in relation to men? 'They have qualities rather than strengths,' G. replied. 'Women are more courageous than men.' In what sense? 'They have more moral courage than men, and indeed more physical courage than men also. If you have to extract a secret by torture, a woman will be more resistant than a man, and undergo greater privations.'

And, presumably, whatever women's defects as you see

them, you must have had many compensations from your friendships with them? 'Certainly, and compensations which have derived from close associations with women – when you need them, and they need you.' Has this happened with many women? 'My successful relationships with women have been few in number. An aspect of the success has been the extent to which they have relied on me for advice. I remember a married woman with whom I was very close telling me that she had had much more consideration from me than she could have had from a husband. This is not, however, surprising. The fact of marriage diminishes the attention a man can give his wife, for he will often measure such attention as a discharge of obligation.'

Perhaps, but today, the Day of Atonement, did you not feel under any obligation to atone for some of your opinions in relation to women? 'My opinions,' G. answered genially, 'certainly classify for inclusion in each of the categories of sin which were enumerated in today's service. Clearly, many of my opinions about women are biased. But they are biased because I am a man, not because I am a particular man.'

Bias, you mean, is inherent in male attitudes towards women? 'There is a built-in bias in most males where women are concerned. If you got on to a train and discovered the driver was a woman, you would have an apprehension that you would not have if the driver was a man. Or, if you set off on a climb and the leader was a woman, you would want much more assurance than if it was a man.'

If all men, or nearly all men, share your biases to some degree, is it not yet another reason to argue that relations between the sexes are not merely tormented but incorrigible? 'When the good Lord established the world, and

Adam and Eve were created, it was established that there would be two different sexes. And since Eve was created from the side of Adam, it could also be said that women were discovered – if that is the right word – later than men.'

But that does not, in itself, imply any moral 'juniority' or inferiority in women, I said. 'If you study the Bible, which I do not,' said G., unyielding, 'the original arrangement was not to have an Eve at all. I cannot think what was the inducement that persuaded God to create her.' As a 'helpmeet' for Adam, said I. 'I do not see why He could not have designed him without the need for further companionship,' said G..

Nevertheless, said I, He did, with all its further consequences, the procreation of the species included. 'The fact that women procreate the race and endure all that is incidental to birth has only a marginal connection with males.' But an important enough connection, said I. 'It is true that males have to fornicate in order for children to be produced,' said G. 'But fornication is a pretty minor process compared with the problems and labour of childbirth. If men had to endure childbirth I do not think anyone would ever be born. The long and thorough-going notice of birth to which women are also subject is a burden which increases the apprehension of it. Men, given similar warning, would not be able to bear it.'

You used the word fornication, which in my ears has the sound of moral reproach. Do you have that sense of it? 'It is merely a word for a process. Copulation might equally do. I think fornication is the right word for a sexual operation involving both sexes.' Do you consider that 'sexual operation' to be an absurdity, or mankind's *summum bonum*, or what? 'Bernard Shaw, in his play *Getting Married*, observed that the sexual process was

sufficiently ridiculous to deserve being judged absurd.'
Perhaps he never experienced it, I said. 'That I do not
know. Whether he remained a virgin all his life must be a
matter of fanciful speculation. His very elaborate descrip-
tions of sexual matters suggest that he did not repine at
keeping his distance from them.' Why do you say that?
'Because he might have found them easier to describe than
to practise,' answered G..

To speak of the sexual act as fornication still sounds to
me as if it were a deadly sin, I said. 'On the contrary. It is
a perfectly natural process. Indeed, the temptation of it
is so potent that very large numbers of people engage in
it.' To the extent that you could condemn an individual
for 'promiscuity' for it, or not? 'Too much importance is
attached to promiscuity, or rather to the reproach of it.
Indeed, promiscuous behaviour is so common that its condemnation can itself become unnatural.'

Does that make you a sexual libertarian? I asked. 'No,
I could be described as a libertarian. I am opposed to
excessive moralising, but I am also less liberal in my view
of sex than most people. I am much more of a prude than
a prig. But I have the sense not to condemn people for
their moral irregularities. I am not opposed to a woman
or a girl having an affair provided that she takes sensible
precautions. My objection is to a flood of illegitimate
children being flung on to society without adequate provision for them; in America, it is almost impossible to find a
Negro who is legitimate.'

But where do you draw the line between the kind of
sexual behaviour you feel able to tolerate morally, and
that which you abhor? 'A high degree of promiscuity is
decadence,' G. replied. 'I would not condemn a woman for
one or two affairs. But if she has an affair weekly it means
she is devoting her life to what she calls, erroneously,

"making love".' Don't you apply the same strictures to men? 'I do not apply the same strictures to men for the reasons that Dr Johnson – a wise old bird – did not. The risk of "confusion in the progeny" is the ground for distinguishing between them,' G. declared.

I expect you must often enough in your life have come across people driven to sexual excess of one kind and another? 'If you are asking me whether there is a shortage of British libertines, that is clearly not the case. The British are less exhibitionist in their sexual activities than the Italians or the French, but they are not less disposed to libertinism,' said G. Did you have evidence of this in your legal practice? 'My practice was very little composed of sex maniacs,' G. answered. 'If they arrived, I would send them away, since I am not equipped to deal with them. I also never liked divorce practice, because of the immensely quarrelsome nature of the proceedings. When marriage partners decide to separate, their first desire is usually to conduct their exchanges on a civilised basis. But within the shortest time such exchanges become homicidal, with the parties tearing lumps of flesh out of each other.'

And what of true love? I asked. Do you imagine that it exists or that it is mere sexual desire, gilded over? 'Love is quite impossible to define, or as difficult to define as is toothache. In both cases, one knows that it is a pain in a certain quarter. Nor can I define what circumstances bring about love, or what is known as love. In my own circle of friends there are men and women who have been married a great number of years. This would argue a strong element of affection in their relationship,' said G., 'but it is very often difficult to discern.'

Are you suggesting that the affection is concealed, or that it is not there? 'What generally happens after a short period of marital bliss,' G. bleakly replied, 'is that the situation produces hostility between them.' That sounds like an *ex-post facto* rationalisation on your part for having avoided marriage. 'That,' G. rejoined, 'is like saying to an animal that it has avoided a trap built for it, when it has merely proceeded along its own path.' No traps were laid for you? 'There were covert plots on certain occasions. But at the time when I might have married I was not regarded as a sufficient prize for such plots to be long-lived.'

Have you ever gone as far as to think the institution of marriage to be absurd *per se*? 'No. But any solemn human activity will be subject to ridicule, and marriage is a particularly appropriate target of it.' Why? 'Because in practice both men and women have to subordinate their personal qualities, sometimes to a large extent, to the marriage relation. If they fail to do so, the marriage will be a failure.'

But why should such subordination of personal qualities be regarded as ridiculous? 'Because the result with which you are often presented is a couple whose individual personalities have been greatly distorted by the relation. That becomes an absurdity.' Nonetheless, you must know some happy marriages where such dire consequences have not occurred? 'Very few, but I have known some.' They do exist? 'Yes, but not in abundance. What I have observed most frequently is that the determination of the spouses has kept their marriages alive. They are limping and halt, but they go on. Among the most humane of laws are the divorce laws,' G. briskly added.

It could also be argued, given the scale of divorce and the numbers of one-parent families, that divorce is too easy, said I. 'That is a simplification,' said G. 'Recourse will only be had to divorce if one or both of the partners desire to be divorced. You cannot blame the desire to be divorced on the law.' But less liberal divorce laws might induce spouses to 'try harder'? 'You can make out an arguable case for such a proposition,' G. replied. 'But if there is a basic difference between the partners which does not heal, it is a social cruelty not to give them the opportunity of terminating the marriage.'

There was once a Chinese emperor who decreed that in his kingdom spouses must divorce after ten years of marriage, unless they wished to retain the bond and applied to a court for permission to do so; the premise of the decree was that a marriage of more than ten years was likely to be oppressive to both parties. 'It was a wise decree,' G. declared. 'In most marriages, given a respectable opportunity of terminating it after ten years, many spouses would seek that opportunity. Moreover, if they knew a termination was coming, they might live more happily in the preceding period.

'The interference of religion in marriage is the cause of more mischief still,' G. continued. 'The view, for instance, that marriage is a *sacrament* would not be comprehensible to most people, and is not comprehensible to me. I can recognise a good honest contract when I see one, but I am not good at recognising *sacraments*. Jews do not often think about sacraments,' G. added; 'I don't think it is part of Jewish theology.' Nevertheless, a Jewish marriage is accompanied with the same kind of religious vows as any other kind of 'consecrated' union. 'Certainly,' declared G. 'There are extracted from the unhappy couple, at the moment when a wine-glass is being ceremonially trodden underfoot, pious undertakings of whose significance they can barely be aware. I consider it to be a shocking waste of wine-glasses.'

I am unsure, said I, whether you think the greater problem with marriage is the institution itself or the fact that men must marry women. 'A determination to sleep in the same bed with the same woman for ever must be regarded as an unreasonable course of conduct. Indeed, it is unnatural to expect two people to remain in the same house and to operate exactly the same regime for ever,' G. declared by way of reply. 'Unless both have other valid interests, it is also rather cruel.'

And if you found yourself on a desert island with a woman, do you think you could stick it for long? I asked. 'I do not think I could stick it for long with any human,' answered G. 'But I would much prefer a woman of taciturn disposition to a talkative male, and prefer a Trappist to both.' Do you mean that you would choose to sit in silence with your desert island companion? 'If I had the company of only one person it would be wise to ration our conversation,' said G. Why? 'Because a continuous exchange of views with the same person would promote such loathing as to excite homicide,' G. replied. 'The ideal companion would be a man who was useful with his hands, and a capable fisherman and carpenter. A woman would be unlikely to have such skills.' Women have other skills of their own. 'Not the fundamental skills which would be required. I would prefer to have a male assistant in building my hut.'

In building your life, do you not think that a female assistant would have helped? 'I would not say that a female assistant might not have been of considerable help. But I have never felt in desperate need of a female assistant.' Never? 'I have not felt the desperate need of it,' G. repeated.

11

Dumplings and
Fraises des Bois

You are a very hospitable person, I said to G. Where would you place hospitality in the moral scheme of things? 'I would regard it as a rather unusual quality,' G. replied. Is it unusual? 'It depends in practice not only upon generosity but the possession of means. It is more difficult to be hospitable if you are penniless; sharing your last crust with someone may constitute an outstanding display of hospitality, but it does not feed the recipient.' Those who are not rich can also be hospitable, said I. 'That is true, but it is much less frequent. Where such hospitality is found it derives from the spirit of generosity alone. To act generously without the means to do so is virtuous, but may be less efficacious,' G. declared with a laugh.

'You have to pay regard also to the quality of Jewish hospitality,' he went on. Is it a distinct thing? 'The hospitality shown by Jews is in general less restrained and inhibited than gentile hospitality, and more widespread among them. The impulse of hospitality in gentiles is attributable largely to rich people. If it comes to the sharing of a last crust, it is more likely to be the characteristic of a Jew than a non-Jew. I cannot speak with knowledge of the Muslims or the Chinese; I understand, however, that the Arabs are very hospitable, but it has to be remembered that the Arabs are semites.'

Are you saying that an hospitable spirit is 'naturally' a Jewish or semitic virtue? 'I do not mean that you find it in every Jew,' G. replied. 'Some of the least hospitable people I have met are Jews. But if you were on the point of setting out to a dinner party and a friend were to arrive unexpectedly at your house whom you wished to take with you, a non-Jewish hostess would feel an immediate objection to having an extra person at her table. Everything will have been planned for the accommodation of a fixed and inflexible number of guests: the plan will take precedence over other considerations, that of hospitality included.'

A Jewish hostess would not react in similar fashion? 'The trait I have mentioned would not be found in traditional Jewish homes. However, it can be found in the homes of some Anglicised Jews, or wherever the most unfortunate characteristics of the English have taken root. Indeed, to be an Anglicised Jew is among the most unhappy of conditions,' G. remarked.

Is it, perhaps, that the English underestimate the moral and social importance of hospitality, rather than that they are inhospitable *per se*? I asked. 'Among the great mass of the English, hospitality is something of which they are apprehensive,' G. replied. 'To them, hospitality entails accepting into their houses people whom they do not know very well. This, for them, constitutes a substantial deterrent.'

But is that not because hospitality is not recognised, or no longer recognised, as a Christian ethical obligation? 'Hospitality is alien to Christian values,' answered G. bluntly. 'Moreover, hospitality is regarded as an obligation only by nice people. Nice people are limited in number in any community, Christian or Jewish. But they are less limited in number in the Jewish community,' said G. Might it be, I asked, that surviving English belief in the more puritanical virtues helps them to justify to themselves their general lack of hospitality to others? 'That is too forced a conclusion,' replied G.. 'What accounts for the paucity of hospitality in England is the national belief in the virtue of keeping yourself to yourself. Hospitality would run counter to such a belief.' Your views about hospitality recall what you said in an earlier conversation about friendship. Is English lack of hospitality related, in your view, to lack of capacity for friendship? 'Both derive, to some extent, from a suspicion in the English of people whom they do not know well. This can be interpreted as revealing either a disinclination for hospitality and friendship or a sensible caution about relationships as such,' G. answered.

I remember my father's frequent complaints that his hospitality to non-Jews was very unevenly reciprocated, or not reciprocated at all, said I. Do you think such complaints were unworthy? 'It was unrealistic of your father to expect reciprocity,' said G. 'The most virtuous hospitality is that which is extended with the least prospect of a reciprocal invitation. To expect an impecunious guest to invite you to the Savoy, or even to his own home, for the purpose of consuming large quantities of caviare and *foie gras* is an unreasonable expectation,' G. said with a laugh. But is the hope of friendly reciprocity morally wrong? I asked. 'It is an ungenerous attitude to adopt. It means that your hospitality is not extended without regard to benefit, but in the hope of obtaining something free from your victim in return,' G. answered.

Have you taken great pleasure in food, whether your own or that of others? I asked G. 'I have never taken great pleasure in food which was madly expensive or distributed on a class basis,' said G. Is food 'distributed on a class basis'? 'You will not find paupers with more than a limited addiction to smoked salmon.' But has food not been one of the great pleasures of your life? 'No. That would be an extravagant, and also a rather unwise, claim to make.' Why? 'Because it would imply gluttony, and hopefully I am not a glutton.' ('I am even more hopeful that I do not entertain many gluttons,' he added.)

Have you ever eaten too much, whether from anxiety or for comfort? 'I do not think that I have any deep anxiety which is either associated with food or allayed by it. If I had such anxiety, it would only show itself, in my case, in concern about where my next meal was coming from. But I have rarely entertained serious doubts about that.'

Can you boil an egg? 'Anyone can boil an egg. Whether I can boil it successfully is another matter.' Do you possess any other culinary skills? 'I have not practised any culinary skills. I have from time to time boiled eggs and made what I alone regard as an omelette; nobody eating it could have considered it as such.' How do you regard culinary skills in others? 'I regard culinary skills as skills properly exercised by women. Probably unfairly, I regard many of the men who excel in such skills as rather effeminate.' Some of London's master chefs might not agree, said I. 'My remark does not include men who have made a great profession of it, like the chefs you mention. Indeed, there is no less reason in principle why a man should have a professional skill in cooking than in book-keeping or stockbroking. The only difference in practice is that the former talent, in some males, will excite a ridicule which may not be entirely unjust. For a man to be dressed in a tall white-linen cap and to adopt, in the kitchen, a didactic attitude towards the rest of mankind about his skill in cooking is in some ways absurd.'

Were you irritated by being called 'Two-Dinners' in *Private Eye*? 'I am never irritated by anything published in *Private Eye* because I have been tutored by experience not to take it seriously. The epithet was a falsehood. It derived from the fact that Max Aitken once arrived late for dinner with me at the Savoy Grill and insisted that I had something more to eat, even though I had already dined. This I did, but he, having a mischievous sense of humour, spiced the belief that I regularly had "two dinners". The whole of the calumny derived from that, but it was not the most serious libel in the world. I have never gone in quest of "two dinners". If I had, there would alway have been in the back of my mind the starving populations of Africa, observing my gluttony,' said G.

Gluttonous or not, why do you think English food is generally so bad? 'Because so many appetites which need to be cultivated to a high point, if food is to be good, remain uncultivated in England. One of the most damaging factors has been the public school system. It has made so many of the middle and upper classes aware early in life that they cannot hope for edible food.' And not hoping for it, they neither expect nor demand it as adults? 'The hope is extravagant, and the reduced expectation self-fulfilling,' G. replied.

If this is so, said I, can you tell a nation's character from what it eats, or likes to eat? 'You can tell important things about a nation from what it eats or likes to eat, but not its character. You can assess the level of its prosperity, for example. But you can tell something of a *man*'s character from what he eats, and from how he eats. The fact that Mr Jones insists on eating three fried eggs, six rashers of bacon and numerous slices of fried bread for breakfast also indicates that he is a man of powerful digestion and equipped with an adequate income to gratify his appetites.'

Yes, but can you judge his soul from such a performance? 'There is no simple rule to judge it by what he consumes. If he chooses to eat caviare and *foie gras* at every meal, it is clear at least that his appetite is determined by his wealth.' You don't believe, as some nineteenth-century materialists believed, that 'man *is* what he eats'? 'Never. If a man has spent his life consuming candles, this would be evidence that he might be an Eskimo,' said G. jovially. 'But I am not convinced that such a taste for candles would have as profound an influence on his character as nineteenth-century materialists might have imagined.' But does a vegetarian, for instance, disclose nothing of his character from his preferences? 'I am inclined to approve vegetarianism since it is a slightly more difficult regime than that adopted by the carnivore. I myself would regard it, on balance, as a commendable aspect of the character of a man.'

In which case, the kinds of food which most of the English most like to eat – chips, baked beans, and the rest of it – should also say something about them? 'I do not regard the appetite as having supreme importance in determining or revealing the nature of the national character,' G. repeated. 'In England, as anywhere, the choice of food depends on many factors, from the length of a man's pocket to his choice of restaurant. This is often a class matter.' The prosperous and discerning can take expensive forms of avoiding action? 'I frequently eat at a very expensive London restaurant, but I do not believe that the food is better there than in other places.' Then why do you eat there? 'Because it is a suitable place to take guests, and is frequented by many of my cronies.'

Do you not have the 'starving populations of Africa' in

mind there, too? 'I do not have any sensation of guilt about the manner in which my life is spent as far as money is concerned. I do not feel guilt sitting in a box at the Opera, even if I believe that the prices of seats should be reduced, and opera made accessible to more people.'

But might not one person reasonably think it a moral weakness for another to eat caviare, or even chocolate ginger? 'It is not a moral weakness. It is a matter of sense, or the absence of it. If a man sits down to tea and eats twelve chocolate éclairs, there will be no doubt that he is either greedy or has been starved of chocolate éclairs for many years. But I would not make a moral judgment of him unless the eating of those chocolate éclairs deprived others of them.'

Nevertheless, you presumably believe that there is a moral virtue in restraining the appetite? 'Not giving way to one's appetites shows a degree of self-control which I could regard as a virtue. The tragedy is that the great mass of mankind cannot gratify its appetites at all, nor even attempt to do so. Indeed, the spread of starvation in the world is so horrifying to recall that it makes the conversation we are having indecent.' Is abstinence then a virtue in itself? 'Yes, in that it negates certain very unfortunate traits in mankind. It negates drunkenness and gluttony, and in that sense is a virtue.'

You inveighed earlier against greed in relation to the accumulation of money, said I. 'Greed applies equally to money, food, clothes, houses, everything,' G. declared; 'if you want to make a splash,' he added obliquely, 'you must take care not to empty the bath.' But, at least in England 'making a splash' is still, in some quarters, deterred by good manners? 'The degree to which greed is restrained is much more relevant than other matters we have discussed in judging national character. If four people are present at tea, and three chocolate éclairs are set down before them, one would hope that, in England, at least one of the four would forswear his éclair. In some countries,' G. continued, breaking into laughter, 'all four would attempt simultaneously to snatch an éclair for themselves. This is not an agreeable trait,' G. added, still laughing. 'Happily, in this country, if you find yourself at table with a group of people who are all English the chance that they will not eat everything before you get your portion is a sufficiently good one.'

Does your hostility to greed imply that you really have an ascetic impulse, whether weak or strong? 'I am reasonably careful about food, I cannot afford to aspire to excessive ostentation, and I do not drink,' G. replied. As a matter of principle, or from personal preference? 'It is not a case of principle,' said G. 'At the beginning of the war, and because the craven enemy would not approach our anti-aircraft guns, we had nothing to do. Drinking in the canteen was the solitary occupation. Doing this made me feel ill, and I decided to give up alcohol until the end of the war. But it would have been a waste of such a sacrificial time if I had resumed drinking. I am now in the position that I do not like it.'

Yet there are other tastes which you surely indulge? 'I have a taste for some Jewish food,' G. replied. 'I prefer Jewish dumplings to non-Jewish dumplings. I have quite a fondness for *gefilte* fish. I think I enjoy some Jewish sausages over *trayfe* sausages, even if, alas, pork sausages cause me no inhibition. I am also very fond of Jewish saveloys, which have a particular flavour.'

You plainly do not fear the effects of cholesterol, said I. 'Many of the foods I like are no doubt lethal, but here I am, nodding at my eightieth birthday, having eaten such items since my fourth or fifth year without fatal effect.'

Would you say you were a gourmand or a gourmet? 'I would not classify myself as either. I am pretty selective about what I eat: I am not very fond of meat, but I am very fond of brisket and the like. When it comes to *entremets* [side-dishes], *fraises des bois* please me greatly. I am not very fond of fish, but I like sardines.'

Would you like to be served wth sardines, brisket and *fraises des bois* when you arrive in heaven? 'If I arrive in heaven, I hope I shall be released from all these hideous human practices.' All of them? 'Giving up food altogether would mean giving up the entire disagreeable digestive process,' G. replied.

12

Serving the Arts

What have you been trying to do, all these years, in the world of the arts? I asked G. 'I have been trying,' he said, 'to stem the taking of retrograde steps in the arts.' What retrograde steps? 'The retrograde steps have generally been the steps taken by influential people in powerful positions who were hostile to the arts, and opposed to them having any finance. It is not even necessary to be hostile to the arts for such opposition to appear; those who are neutral towards the arts will also frequently display it,' G. added.

Have these steps grown more numerous or less in the course of your efforts? 'They are always numerous. But they became more numerous when a Conservative government was elected in 1979. Thereafter, the bipartisan policy of giving support to the arts was deliberately abandoned, and speeches could be heard in the House of Commons opposing any grants to the arts whatever. These speeches have been the expression of simple prejudice, which in the recent years of Tory government it has become quite acceptable to voice. In Jennie Lee's day, no one would have dared attack the arts in the House of Commons.' Did such opposition, in your judgment, flow from a lack of interest in the arts, or from some other cause? 'It flowed from a certainty that opposition to arts funding would have mass support,' G. replied.

Why should such opposition have mass support? 'It rests upon the fact that the number of people interested in the arts in Britain is tiny in proportion to the population as a whole.' Why should this be? 'The basic reason is lack of understanding of the arts. Understanding requires intellectual effort, and precious few are capable of it.' Perhaps, but lack of interest or understanding is one thing, opposition another, said I. 'Opposition derives from the uneducated suspicion, sustained by the power of the tabloids, that the arts are leftish, effeminate and homosexual. Such suspicions are strongest among the worst-educated working class in Western Europe. The opinions to which these suspicions give rise are valid opinions; they are not respectable opinions, but they are easily found.'

Are all such suspicions of the same kind? 'No. Everyone who has the suspicions to which I have referred has a distinct belief about what the leading vice of the arts is. Some people identify this vice as an unacceptable rejection, by the arts and by artists, of authority and order.' For them the 'Lords of Misrule' lurk in the art world? 'It is more that the art world does not conform to their idea of discipline, a defect which the British hate.'

But don't the English admire eccentricity? 'As a general proposition, that is not so. Eccentricity arouses alarm, especially in more orthodox minds. Such admiration of eccentricity as there is usually coincides with admiration of longevity. An aged eccentric is more acceptable than a young one. Youthful eccentricity, especially if artistic, is not in general regarded with great favour.'

And do you think that others might see the arts as expressive of emotions which are best left hidden? 'Anything which expresses deep feeling is regarded with grave suspicion by the English. But I do not think the arts are individual in this respect,' G. replied. 'The principal problem, as anyone concerned with the arts must realise, is that most of the British people are not interested in the arts at all. The effort to cultivate a larger interest may be compared with the labours of Sisyphus. No sooner do you get the stone some way up the hill, than back it rolls.' Art, then, is an inert mass, with a tendency to roll down the hill if not prevented? 'True,' said G. 'It is a simplification to say so, but not a remote simplification. If you do not maintain the right propaganda and sustain the right effort on behalf of the arts, you will gain an inch and lose a foot. That is a measure of distance,' G. added, 'not a surgical disaster.' You are not claiming to have been pushing this stone alone? 'Not alone. But there is always insufficient assistance to ensure that the stone reaches the hill-top.'

Nevertheless, you have already declared, in effect, that you would rather have been pushing this stone uphill than serving as a Lord Justice of Appeal. 'Yes, because despite the difficulties it is still possible to get something done in the arts by well-directed effort.' Can't a Lord Justice of Appeal, in his own sphere, do the same? 'All you can do as a Lord Justice of Appeal is try to operate an inadequate legal system,' G. replied dismissively.

What is this 'something' that you can get done in the arts? 'You can stimulate artistic activity, which I rate more important than serving the legal system.' Does this mean that you would rather have been an artist than a solicitor? 'I would rather have been anything than a solicitor,' G. replied with a laugh. 'But I have never had any pretensions to be an artist. You have to have a God-given talent, which, alas, I have not got. When I gave up the violin there was a sigh of relief among the neighbours; my painting at school was the most derided in the school's history. My interest in the arts has always been as a spectator. But the spectator's role is itself most important. The spectator provides the audience, buys the tickets and furnishes the applause. It is a role which is basic to the continuance of the arts and the survival of the artist.'

To go back a moment, why is it more important to stimulate artistic activity than to serve the legal system? Do you mean that the former is a morally superior activity, or what? 'It is a matter of personal choice, but no one believes that serving the legal system is a sacred cause.' Is not justice sacred? 'Justice may be sacred, but serving the legal system is not synonymous with serving justice. It may often be synonymous with serving injustice. The encouragement of the arts is an undoubted element in procuring the existence of a civilised society.' So, too, is the administration of justice, is it not? 'The administration of justice is supportive of civilisation, but it has less obvious effects,' G. replied.

Does it? 'It has different effects. I would not say anything to encourage people to lawlessness. It is evident that the enforcement of law prevents anarchy and keeps us safe from individual violence. No amount of support for the arts can secure this. If a man is about to mug you,' G. added, beginning to laugh, 'it is no good playing him Beethoven's Seventh Symphony. It won't stop him,' said G. with great hilarity. I doubt if it has been tried, said I. 'No, but there is a school of thought that believes music can cure insanity,' said G., still laughing.

I still cannot gather, I said, what manner of philosophy guided you in rolling your 'stone' up the hill. 'I had the same simplistic philosophy as Jennie Lee,' G. replied. 'It is that the arts are good for people. She was admirably frank in saying that she knew very little about the arts and was only seriously introduced to them when she became Minister of the Arts. Her belief was that, deprived of the arts, society is reduced to a primitive level.'

It can be reduced to a primitive level even with the arts: there were Nazis who liked Beethoven's string quartets. 'That is the sort of contradiction,' G. replied sharply, 'which will enable you to disprove any proposition whatever. The fact that unworthy persons engage in worthy pursuits does not discredit the pursuits themselves. Moreover, I do not think that you will find that the Nazis were overwhelmingly dedicated to the arts, even if there are rumours that Hitler loved the music of Wagner. But then I do not find Wagner to be the best exponent of a humane artistic philosophy,' G. added. No, but the larger point is that art and primitivism, Beethoven and Buchenwald, may go together. 'That is merely to say that in any human society evil things live side by side with good things. It does not make the good things bad nor the evil things good.'

Is the implication of what you are saying, though you have not declared it outright, that the taste of the *hoi polloi* requires to be guided by the cultured? 'In relation to many people, taste does require to be guided. But that is no more than to believe that education needs to be guided by teachers; this is a general belief which explains why navvies are not enrolled as schoolmasters. Unfortunately, great numbers block their ears to guidance in the arts.' Is that surprising? 'It ought not to be.' Why? 'Because in order to be surprised it would be necessary to suppose that everybody is interested in the arts. That would be a piece of massive self-deception,' G. declared. But who is deceived? I asked. Is there not a general understanding about this? 'There may be,' G. replied, 'but people continue to deceive themselves in their expectations.'

Are you saying, then, that we inhabit some kind of

philistine wasteland? 'It would be fairer to describe Britain as an uneducated nation,' G. replied. 'Moreover, to say that it was "philistine" could be considered an undeserved reproach of the Philistines,' added G., with his customary levity. 'I am not aware that any survey of Philistine IQs was carried out in biblical times to justify the application of such an epithet to Britain; the Philistines may have been greatly cultivated people.' But the British in general are not? 'There are many agencies in the arts and an enormous activity of concerts, operas, plays and art exhibitions, but the great mass of the population is not interested in art,' G. repeated. 'It would require a team of very strong horses to drag an average group of our fellow-citizens to a performance of Wagner's *Ring*.'

Should they be condemned for their resistance? 'They are not to be condemned provided that they recognise, whatever their own tastes, that performances of art are significant and need to take place, even if they do not choose to attend them. But it is also a fact that many of these same people, while not requiring, or avoiding, the arts for themselves, are often keen that their children should have some knowledge of them. Their own abandonment of the arts is more than neutralised by their concern that their children should play a musical instrument, go to art galleries, read books and so forth. All these things will be desired even by the most ignorant and insensitive of parents, so long as some voice which they respect is urging the importance of the arts to them. It is therefore exceptionally important that school-teachers should be groomed into possessing a knowledge of the arts which they can impart to their pupils.'

Is this not the struggle of art with what some, at least, call philistinism? I asked. 'It is more a struggle of art against apathy,' G. answered. 'If you were to stop any thousand people in the street and try to persuade them into a performance of serious music, their responses would be vigorous and might endanger your life.' But why on earth would the apathetic bother to attack you physically in the cause of the arts? 'Because there would be apathy in their lack of understanding of the arts, but violence in their reaction to your efforts to overcome it,' G. said with a laugh.

Would you not concede that there are pains as well as pleasures in becoming 'cultured'? 'In order that a person should enjoy opera and other serious music there will certainly be occasions when he must hear it *malgré lui*, and when it may cause him pain. Moreover, one of the important British freedoms is freedom from art. You cannot drag a man handcuffed and in leg-irons to a performance of Wagner. The rattling of his chains and his cries for help would disturb the performance.' Have you ever heard cries for help at a performance of the *Ring*? 'No, and I have never seen people in leg-irons either,' G. replied with great merriment. 'But I have seen people who looked as if they were in leg-irons. On two occasions I have persuaded newspaper tycoons – one of them Lord Thomson, and the other will remain nameless – to attend concerts. In the first case, he had never been to a concert in his life, the programme was designed to torture, and I could sense the pain the man was undergoing. In the second case, the tycoon left at the interval, and I was glad to see him go. His visible suffering would have been intolerable to any humane person.'

But if some music causes people such pain, isn't there a sense in which it is *bad* music? I asked. 'The fact that some people don't like something doesn't make it bad. It might make it pretentious or unintelligible, but not necessarily bad.' Nevertheless, those who suffer pain in their encounters with some forms of culture or art are likely to think that those who derive pleasure from them must be snobs? 'They may think so,' G. replied. 'It could also be said that many people go to Covent Garden out of a motive of snobbery. But if they went year after year to the *Ring*, their motive could only be masochistic.'

Does the *Ring* cause you pain too? 'No, it does not cause me pain; sections of it, although only sections, give me delight.' Why then do you keep using it as your negative example? 'Because it is the best illustration of something which is, on the whole, in regular supply but which would arouse no great pleasure in unartistic people.' Is that a judgment in any way influenced by Wagner's reputation as an anti-semite? 'Not in the slightest. It is madness to allow a man's prejudices to prevent you from enjoying his music; you would be depriving yourself to no purpose.'

To quote Montaigne, said I, 'let us go further into this matter since here we are.' When Ikey, the old clothesman, or some other Jewish stereotype, steps on to the page of a Victorian novel, how do you respond? 'A good instance is Trollope,' G. replied. 'His pages are permeated with anti-semitism. It is often concealed as a sentiment against "foreigners", but it is inadequately concealed. I remember a passage in one of his novels where a young Jew – plainly a Jew, but not specified as such – comes to present a proposal to a barrister, who conceals his anti-semitism by asking, "Are you an Englishman?"' But you yourself said to me some weeks ago that you were 'not an Englishman', I remarked. 'I do not regard myself as an Englishman, but unlike Trollope's character I was not objecting to that fact, merely recording it,' G. declared.

To return to Ikey, said I: every cultivated Jew has had to encounter him and his like in English literature, and not infrequently either. 'You would have to have a very limited literary experience not to have come across examples of the anti-semitic kind you mention,' agreed G. 'There is a good deal of it in Agatha Christie and John Buchan also, for instance.' To say nothing of Chesterton and Belloc. 'They were notorious anti-semites because they were both Catholics.' Are you saying that Catholics are by definition anti-semitic? 'You are more likely to find it in Catholics,' G. replied, 'because early in life Catholics are taught that Christ was "killed by Jews".'

When you come to anti-semitic comment or innuendo in a work of literature do you stumble over it, or do you say to yourself 'The author is a good writer, one must read on'? 'It does not harm a good novel because you will be carried along by the sweep of the writing. Moreover, in Trollope you do not have the impression that the anti-semitism is inspired by a desire to do injury, but by what he genuinely believed; he lived in a period when anti-semitism was a sentiment often encountered. Nor do I feel that Trollope was governed by this sentiment to an obsessive degree, even if I should not want to sanitise his novels in my own mind by erasing all response to his offensive references to the Jews.'

Do you share the preoccupation of some Jews with the effect upon audiences of *The Merchant of Venice*? 'The character of Shylock was the creation of a man who had probably never met a Jew. Shakespeare was reflecting beliefs as to what a Jew was which were prevalent at the time. But the depiction of Shylock, if analysed, is by no means offensive. The great speech in which the question is asked, "If you prick us, do we not bleed?" is a vindication of pride in one's race.'

We were speaking earlier of serious music; now we are speaking of serious drama. What does this word 'serious' mean? Is there, for example, music which is 'unserious'? 'It is a waste of time to define them,' G. replied. 'The difference between them can only be sensed. But serious music is certainly music which will keep a lot of people away from any concert hall in which it is performed. If performed on radio or television it will similarly cause large numbers to switch off their sets or change channels, in favour of Mr Wogan or some other contemporary delight.'

Nevertheless, as you would yourself admit, there are many places of serious musical resort, like the Royal Opera House, which are often full. Does that mean nothing? 'The fact that the Royal Opera House is full does not mean anything.' Why not? 'It is, as I have said, a centre of snobbery, where people go to look at and despise those who are poorer than themselves, and to admire others for being richer. It makes no serious contribution to the arts,' G. declared roundly. Nevertheless, you often go there yourself, said I. 'It is true that I maintain an outrageously expensive box at Covent Garden, which I share with five other people.' Despite your criticisms? 'It provides personal satisfaction to the relatively few individuals who can derive continuous pleasure from attending a succession of great operas.' What about Pavarotti in Hyde Park? I interrupted. 'The following for Pavarotti is a social peculiarity,' G. replied, 'and it was not a proper use of Hyde Park. But in disseminating interest among plebeians, the Royal Opera House does nothing. They could only get into the place if they broke in.'

Is this the kind of thing which, in your estimation, gives culture a bad name? 'Of course it does. Nevertheless, there is available to people in this country a very large amount of satisfying cultural material, some of which is free. They can go to the National Gallery, the Tate, the Wallace

Collection and a great number of other places; they can spend a fortnight in the British Museum and no charge is made. The spread of interest in classical music which has developed in my lifetime has been enormous, for which the major credit must go to the BBC. The Proms, for instance, where young people stand for hours listening to music, make a substantial contribution to the arts, which the Royal Opera House does not. It is only when a snob element is introduced, as it is at Covent Garden, that culture exposes itself to reproach.'

Is such reproach justified? I asked. Is not 'high art' expensive, and for that reason, among others, also exclusive? 'If so,' G. replied, 'it is equally true of *haute cuisine* or high cooking. Eating caviare is bound to be exclusive for two reasons: on account of its cost, and because there are people who do not like it. In the case of opera, I cannot see how some of the expense and exclusivity is to be avoided if you are going to mount performances whose price is determined by the insane fees paid to the performers. If the management of an opera house thinks there is virtue in persuading an overweight Pavarotti to sing *Tosca*, there will always be the need for enormously high charges. As an actor, a polar bear would have given a better performance, but he sings like an angel.' G. broke into laughter. 'However, it would give me a rude shock if, on arrival in heaven, I was to find that all the angels looked like Pavarotti.'

Laughter here stopped our conversation for some moments. You were talking about the high charges at the opera, I resumed. 'Yes, and such charges can only be paid by the wealthy, when the wealthy are the worst equipped to appreciate the arts.'

Is there any necessary connection between wealth and an incapacity to appreciate the arts? 'If the wealthy are also inadequately educated there is a connection,' G. answered. 'The worst offenders in relation to the arts are those who have achieved material success without education. Even when they can be described as "self-educated", they often believe they have attained their wealth by the strength of their own right arms, and would have been handicapped by education. There have been many occasions when I have attended dinner parties given by tycoons and been really wounded by their sentiments on matters which concern me. But they are rarely conscious of it. On the other hand, the richest man I know is also the most discerning collector of paintings whom I know. He is not a man with whom one could have a conversation on a philosophical or intellectual subject, but he has an amazing eye for a picture.'

There is a saying in Yiddish, I remarked, that 'whatever a man has for an eye, so he sees'. What kind of an eye has he? 'It is an eye for a valuable picture.' Then his motive is that of cupidity rather than aesthetic desire? 'No. His world is bounded by money standards, and he would not buy a painting which was not expensive. He would not ransack the stalls for a rare engraving. He has no interest in purchasing modern art because he cannot be sure of it. But when he is supported by his own judgment about the quality of a painting – a Rembrandt, a Titian, a Rubens – and by the established practice of others, he will buy.'

Does it make him a cultured man in any sense which has meaning? 'It makes him a man who has an understanding of art.' But in what sense is he cultured? 'In the sense that he gives support to the market for traditional art.' Does that make him cultured? 'It does not make him extensively cultured. He understands a part of culture.'

How would you define a cultured person? 'A cultured person is someone who is prepared to sacrifice time on intellectual activities,' G. replied. But that surely indicates only a readiness to be cultured, not the achievement of it, said I. 'If a man is articulate, selective in his opinions, and devotes his time to worthwhile occupations, that is the beginning of culture,' G. said. Is there not more to it than that? 'There is more to it. Culture has a general meaning, but it has particular contents and many aspects. It is shaped by home background, reading, school and other influences. All these things coalesce to make a cultured person. But if you were shipwrecked on a desert island and you were able to read the ship's library which had been cast upon the shore with you, provided that it was reasonably stocked, that would itself be a means to becoming cultured.' Would it be enough? 'No. A fully cultured individual is interested in literature, in music, in theatre, in pictures, in dance.'

But can you be cultured without being moral? I asked. 'I do not think culture is synonymous with morality.' You can be a cultured man and a villain? 'Oh yes,' said G. 'There are many instances of cultured villains.' Is an antique-dealing shark who can spot a Sheraton at two hundred paces a man of culture? 'His eye is trained to deprive you of your valuable dining-chairs for a song. Most burglars also have a good eye for valuable property. In fact, it is a mistake to enter the trade of burglary without a capacity to discriminate between what is valuable and what is not. A jewel thief would be ill advised to practise the trade if he could not distinguish between a diamond and a piece of glass.'

Yes, but does such connoisseurship qualify the man who possesses it for the title 'cultured'? 'If he uses his knowledge and discrimination for the purposes of theft one must regard it as unworthy knowledge.' A cultured person is a worthy person? 'A cultured person is a worthier person than an uncultured or ignorant person.' Yet you said just now that there are 'many cultured villains'. 'There are, but a burglar whose knowledge enables him to burgle with rapid decision and expert selection is much more a villain than a man of culture.' Because it is a moral quality to be cultured? 'It is a moral thing to be *educated*.' Why? 'Because it involves effort which may not be rewarded.'

Let us return to the 'stone' of culture which you have been rolling up-hill. Did it roll back again because of hostility to artistic experiment and innovation as such? 'Certainly. If you went to the Arts Council in my day, a considerable number of its own employees, who were supposed to propagate the cause of the arts, had a hostility to any innovative art whatever. But they were overcome by the determination of the people at the top to see that innovative art was given a fair chance. However, in consequence, they had to deal with absurdities, as when a special committee was set up to deal with new ideas. It would sit in solemn discussion about whether a play performed by actors on their hands and knees was worthy of support,' said G.

What other forms of opposition did you encounter? 'Mary Whitehouse, for example, came to see me when I was Chairman of the Arts Council in order to complain that young people were flocking to see "pornographic plays" in theatres supported by the Arts Council. During my exchanges, I said to her, "Madam, are you aware of the tens of thousands of young people who fill concert halls, attend art galleries, visit museums and so on?" "I am not interested in them," she replied; "I am concerned about the pornographic plays which the Arts Council is subsidising." "Your mind," I said to her, "is glued to the gutter."'

Did she have any general ground for complaint, in your

judgment? 'Occasionally, directors of plays have a penchant for showing people taking their clothes off. Few of us believe that a performance is enhanced by the sight of nakedness. If, however, you had a play about cannibals it would be surprising if the directors were to put the actors into morning coats and top-hats. But in Mrs Whitehouse's case, it was evident to me that she saw pornography everywhere. There are some people who wear rose-tinted spectacles and see everything rose-coloured; her spectacles were coloured in whatever hue pornography could be said to have.'

Yes, but did she have cause to complain, do you think, about certain forms of theatrical innovation? 'Mrs Whitehouse was not complaining about innovation but about lewdness. She probably had some cause for complaint by her standards. But her standards were not my standards. Moreover, I have a horror of censorship, but for her "censorship" is the most musical of sounds.'

But why should anyone be expected to appreciate the simulation of homosexual rape in *The Romans in Britain* or of the stoning of an infant in *Saved*? 'The only way you can excuse such things,' G. declared, 'is by saying that what a man can think of must bear expression. This proposition must be modified by the fact that certain forms of such expression are sickening. But one must face the truth that most people's dreams, including the dreams of artists, express what they want. The fact that I personally would find it difficult to have the lewd, obscene or violent dreams which some art wishes to express does not mean that their expression by others must be prohibited. If you were to hear me in my bedroom you would judge from my tranquil snores that I was having peaceful dreams, or no dreams at all,' G. added.

But is there any virtue – moral, artistic, intellectual – in appreciating the matters we have mentioned? I asked. 'There is a degree of horror which must be unacceptable even to the most libertarian of individuals. No claim of artistic necessity can justify a performance in which a man's limbs are torn off,' G. jocularly declared. 'However, I have been involved in observing a wide variety of extreme artistic performances for years, but I have never seen anyone's limbs being torn off in front of me.'

Perhaps, but are no bounds therefore to be set? 'Take *The Romans in Britain*. I was roped in to give evidence for the defence in the case which was brought against it. Its attackers had decided that they would regard what was enacted in the play not as simulated for theatrical purposes but as a real sexual assault. I was not called. But, if I had been, I would have said that I had never seen any dramatic performance which was a "real happening". In fact, such a thing would defeat the whole purpose of a play as a theatrical representation.'

Nevertheless, the logic of your objections during a previous conversation to 'excessive moralising' is surely that you should also dislike excessive 'immoralising'? 'No,' G. replied flatly. 'Moreover, such issues cannot be determined by like or dislike. The fact that you or I dislike something should not lead to its being banned to the rest of humanity.' But this is not a satisfactory answer for the Mary Whitehouses of the world, said I. 'I think it is a complete answer to the Mary Whitehouses of the world. She would not admit that there is any merit in anything which, to her, is "obscene" or "pornographic". On such a ground, she would have been on the side of every enemy of literature over the ages. She would have denounced Shaw's *Widowers' Houses* and been in hot pursuit of poor Oscar Wilde. As for *Lady Chatterley's Lover*, I doubt whether she would have survived the shock of reading it when it was first published.'

Do you dislike censorship more than you dislike most of the matters which might, under some regimens, be censored? 'No, that is not correct. I dislike censorship; how much I like, or dislike, the matters which under some regimens might be censored is unimportant. The suppression of what can be thought about, and therefore written about or otherwise depicted, is of no benefit to mankind.'

However that may be, Mrs Whitehouse's form of objection to artistic or imaginative excess could be considered the preoccupation of a relatively small minority, said I; objection to novelty as such and suspicion of artistic snobbery may or may not be equally uneducated but they surely differ in scale and kind? 'Yes. But a very large part of the hostility they express is that a play, a book, or a piece of music is unintelligible to the individual concerned.' Should not the arts be intelligible even to the uninstructed, to the man-in-the-street? 'No more than a Greek drama in the original would be,' G. replied swiftly.

But do you allow that genuine moral or intellectual scruple might enter into objections to some forms of artistic expression? 'Certainly. You can object to something because it outrages your beliefs or your intelligence. But there will always be a greater suspicion of anything that people cannot understand. If you were now to set out to propagate Einstein's Theory of Relativity there would be the gravest suspicion of it,' he chuckled. 'People would say that Einstein was a German, or that he had failed to shake off his Nazi associations,' G. declared with heavy irony. 'Suspicion and false condemnation are customarily directed at whatever is beyond the understanding of the suspicious. Indeed, it is fortunate that so many great philosophers, writers and artists never achieved popular estimation in their own days. If they had, we would now believe that Spinoza kept mistresses and that Heine was a homosexual.'

Do you mean that there is a popular animus against cultivation itself? 'There is animus against what people cannot understand and do not want for themselves. If you were to say that you attended a concert in the Festival Hall or the Royal Albert Hall every night of the week, or merely once a week, there are many who would regard you with the greatest suspicion and probably consider you a liar.' Why a liar? 'Because whatever their limited experience of a classical music concert, it is likely to have seemed an agony, in which untuneful works were deliberately played to their great distress. They would not believe that you could submit yourself regularly to the expense of it, or to submit yourself to it at all.'

Have you ever thought, then, in your box at the Opera, that 'art for the masses' might in general be a contradiction? ' "Art for the masses" can mean anything,' G. replied. 'It can mean musical performances by a brass band. If it plays tolerable tunes, that is also art for the masses. Nor would I quarrel with a man who chooses to spend a Saturday afternoon watching Tottenham Hotspur play Manchester United; it is a perfectly reasonable way to spend a Saturday afternoon. He could, of course, spend it reading a classical Greek drama in the original,' G. added sardonically. 'Indeed, I would not claim that interest in sport is inconsistent with an interest in the arts. It is not inconsistent to engage in both intellectual and popular pursuits. I can, perhaps inappropriately, instance myself: I love watching cricket. Nor could I say with total conviction that I would prefer listening to a modern musical composition to attending a cricket match at Lord's.'

But despite your own catholicity of taste, there is a considerable public recoil from 'high art' on the grounds, however vulgar, that it is the property of 'privilege' or of an 'élite'? 'This attitude exists,' G. replied. 'But it is merely used to justify a hostility which is directed against whatever people do not want, or cannot understand.' That may be, I said, but hasn't the art which smacks of bourgeois culture, or culture with a capital K, always been disliked by some people on class, or pretendedly class, grounds?

'I do not myself share Goering's desire for a revolver whenever the word culture is mentioned,' G. replied. 'Even if I had a revolver – I surrendered it at the end of the war – I should not want to shoot anyone for anything. The criticism of culture which you mention is generally the work of small groups of malcontents who would like to rationalise their hostilities in that way.' Are they right to detect class snobbery in some artistic pursuits? In attendance at Glyndebourne, for example? 'I do not think snobbery is entirely the correct word for it.' You used it yourself of Covent Garden, which you called 'a centre of snobbery', said I. 'Snobbery is only part of it. Even if access is limited to a few people who have acquired the taste for it, some of whom go because they think it redounds socially to their credit, none of them can escape the artistic quality of it, nor can all of them be condemned on class grounds. To have a lot of dukes writhing in pain together at an operatic performance is not a common occurrence,' G. added.

Nevertheless, it seems to me that there is intense plebeian hostility towards culture, whenever such culture is seen as the private province of an élite, said I: élitism has become this kind of vulgarity's most frequently employed term of abuse. 'Such hostility undoubtedly exists, and is increased where people believe that "their money" is being spent on it. Indeed, a tiny sum is. But the penny-ha'penny per person which was spent each year when I was Chairman of the Arts Council was well spent. If the amount has increased since then, it is no evidence of enlightenment on the part of the government, which shows little approbation for the arts.'

The present government is not, to your mind, the friend of art and culture? 'I doubt if we have ever had a government of such pitiful intellectual material as the present one. We even have a prime minister who has boasted that he did not go to university. If you were provided with a list of the favourite reading matter of the members of the present cabinet you would certainly be shocked. In the days of Gladstone and other well-educated statesmen of the past, the classical authors would often have appeared on such a list. I doubt whether any of the present government can read Latin, let alone Greek.' Is Greek neded to make a man wise? 'Greek is not required to make a man wise, because the Almighty furnishes wisdom. But it is desirable for a man to know Greek if he is to be properly educated. Although I had a lot of Latin, I had no Greek and feel at a disadvantage that the whole area of Greek thought and sensibility is removed from my knowledge.'

You are not saying that knowledge of Greek should be a precondition for admission to a British government? 'If it was, there would be no government at all. But it would be a better precondition to have absorbed principles from Greek political philosophy which are relevant to states-manship, than to possess a familiarity with the novels of Jeffrey Archer, which I am sure is their standard reading. The Prime Minister has told the world that Archer is the only man he trusts. I do not question that he is worthy of trust but what is surprising is that he should occupy such an exclusive fiduciary and literary position, especially with a prime minister.'

I have never read a Jeffrey Archer novel, said I. Have you? 'I have not,' G. replied, 'and I expect your literary experiences have also been denuded of Ruby M. Ayres and Barbara Cartland.' In my case, of John Mortimer also. 'The ones I have mentioned touch bottom,' said G. 'John Mortimer is a different matter. He is a populariser. These people are vulgarisers.'

Some might regard our exchanges to be as snobbish as others would consider the audiences at Covent Garden or Glyndebourne to be. They would insist that a Jeffrey Archer novel was as much part of the culture as any. 'It is part of the culture. The culture comprises everyone who writes anything at all. But a man cannot be blamed for having a selective and educated mind. Such a mind will get no satisfaction out of Jeffrey Archer. Conversely, a man who had devoted his life to brass-rubbing might consider himself to be a cultured person for that reason. I would not; just as I would not consider a man who was thoroughly conversant with every type of butterfly to be thereby a thoroughly educated person.' The brass-rubber and butterfly expert, however, might themselves consider the world of private views, art committees and first nights to be a world of artifice, not art. 'Yes, but there is fortunately a large enough artistically-minded population – although it constitutes only a tiny percentage of the population as a whole – whose concern with the arts is not artifice, and who really want to attend theatres, listen to concerts and visit exhibitions for their own sake.'

But if the 'snob' can be duped by his or her own artistic pretensions, have not many others who are not snobs been duped by much contemporary artistic fashion? 'The word "duped" would presuppose that there was an intention to dupe, a *mens rea*. Are you duped by that painting?' G. asked, pointing to a 'blue period' Picasso on his wall. 'Artists do what they can and sometimes more than they can, but I do not think anyone is duped by the results. An unwarranted enthusiasm for a particular work of art is more likely to be the result of self-deception than of artistic merit,' G. wryly added.

The Tate's pile of bricks was not, then, a duping of the public? 'No one dupes you if a pile of bricks is presented as a pile of bricks, although it is difficult to see why anyone should do it. You have not been deceived. Indeed, an ordinarily sane person could not be brought to believe that a pile of bricks was a work of art; if he believed it fervently he would be certifiable. Moreover, if a gallery is persuaded that a pile of bricks is an artistic object it is perfectly entitled to try to persuade others of it, even though you or I might think that those who assemble a pile of bricks in order to excite the spectator's aesthetic emotions should be hanged; or, to be more lenient, flogged.' What you are actually doing, said I, is good-humouredly shrugging your shoulders, and declaring that there is no accounting for taste. 'I think that is a healthy attitude,' said G. 'Moreover, it is better than denouncing something when one can never be on secure ground.'

But have you never, in these last years, felt dismay or disbelief at what has been presented to your gaze as an art object? 'There have been many times when I have believed that someone has produced a piece of nonsense which he wants me to think is worthy of my attention.' In which case, it would not be surprising if the average man, lacking your knowledge and phlegm, thought such things to be merely impositions and pretences?

'He would take them as symptoms of decadence, and he might well be right,' G. conceded. 'What makes it more difficult is that these absurdities are informed by total sincerity. When I was Chairman of the Arts Council, I visited an artistic exhibition which consisted of a large number of catfish swimming about in a tank, and which were being culled once or twice a day by electrocution. The only intention was that, having been killed, the catfish would be offered to the public to be eaten in muffins. I sent to the artist to ask him what all this depicted. He said that life was hard and cruel, and that this was the best way of showing it. I replied that life was only hard and cruel for a catfish if it fell into the hands of a demented Californian artist. He took great offence and said that he would report me to the American ambassador.'

While not much light was shed on the world by his catfish, or by the Tate's bricks, or by the silences of John Cage, do the more conventional forms of artistic expression illuminate our times? Does anyone, for instance, really have to attend the productions of the National Theatre to gain insight into the moral and other dilemmas of the day? 'The National Theatre,' G. answered, 'provides a vigorous indication of theatrical taste, and has had significant dramatic successes. The last play I saw there – Priestley's *An Inspector Calls* – was mawkish beyond belief. Nevertheless, people who attend the National Theatre's productions can derive both interest and entertainment from them.'

But is it the place to go to obtain insights into the sensibility of our age? Indeed, why should anyone now attend the theatre for such a purpose? 'It is valuable to go to the theatre, I do not necessarily say to the National, but it is valuable to go.' Why? 'First, because it is a harmless way of spending time which might otherwise be occupied in less harmless ways. Second, because there is to be found in the legacy of the theatre the expressions of some of the most distinguished minds of all time. A really successful dramatist, even if not a great thinker, will almost certainly convey sentiments which are valuable, insofar as they are novel and entertaining to their audience.'

But surely the theatre is no longer the arena in which the great moral conflicts of the time are publicly rehearsed? 'I disagree. They may be inadequately presented, but they are presented for all that. It should also be remembered that if a play is not entertaining nobody will attend it merely to have his morality improved on a diet of boredom. People will avoid going to any kind of artistic activity which is too didactic, or in which the morality is too obvious. Moreover, Shakespeare, who was a marvellous poet, did not himself rehearse the great moral conflicts of his time. It is not a great *moral* loss, whatever other loss it might be, not to hear a performance of Shakespeare's plays. If you analyse them they are in general anything but moral. Take *Hamlet*, for example. Almost everyone in it, virtuous or otherwise, comes to a sticky end.'

That may be so, but can it be claimed that at the National Theatre the audience is regularly, or at all, wrung to its withers in confrontation with the great problems of the day, moral or any other? 'I think the National Theatre has, overall, done well. People are encouraged to go there for the sake of going. Unlike at Covent Garden it is open to almost everyone to buy some sort of ticket. A fixed disinclination to do so at the National Theatre could only come about where an individual has been inadequately educated. It does a representative sample of the British drama, from Shaw and Priestley to Pinter or Alan Bennett. Pinter is a good example of a contemporary playwright who thinks that he is tackling the great problems of the day.' But surely any theatre which considers Pinter its doyen, or even one of its doyens, must have lost its way?

'His notion of a great problem of the day is one, for example, in which there is a sexual triangle. Such a diagnosis may not be mine,' said G., 'but if a play is too moralising it becomes quickly tedious.'

That is not my point, I said. It is that the theatre has surely ceased to be the forum in which the community, through its playwrights, faces itself and sees its profoundest dilemmas and challenges articulated on its behalf, as in the time of the Greeks. 'In the time of the Greeks,' G. replied, 'the entire community could get into one forum. Today, to get 50 million people into a single building would tax the ingenuity of the best of modern architects.'

What form, then, would your artistic utopia take? I asked. Would it be one in which a mass audience had mass access to the arts? 'No,' said G., 'it would be one in which a large number of the population was educated to a wish to have access to the arts.' With redeeming effect? 'That is altogether too moralistic a view. But I believe that once you have won a young person to the arts there is no danger of his joining a street gang and taking part in a racist attack. Having made that statement,' G. added, 'I await a phone-call from a magistrate telling me that he has an artistic person before him on a criminal charge, and asking me for my comments.'

But you said earlier that the arts could not 'keep us safe from violence' and that it was no use playing Beethoven to a mugger? 'There is no contradiction. Once you have interested a young man in any decent activity he is unlikely to be lost to crime or decadence. An individual who attends every Promenade concert very rarely features at the Old Bailey.' Is he morally too refined, or merely too busy? 'His preoccupation with virtuous activities does not allow him the time for provoking trouble. It is very rare to find a chess champion who is also a professional burglar,' G. added.

Nevertheless, it is plain that you do not like the suggestion that the arts are in some way 'redeeming', or a form of salvation? 'The arts should be spared an obvious morality. They have their own moral message. I do not think that the artist should set out with a deliberate moral purpose.' My point is different, I said: has not your young person 'won to the arts' been 'redeemed' or 'saved' in any moral sense? In your own activities in the arts did you proceed on an assumption no more moral than that, like a fibrous diet, they are 'good for you'?

'It was never my objective to redeem mankind from anything,' G. replied. 'I would regard such an objective as an unwarranted intrusion into its liberties.' Does this mean that mankind can go to the devil if it wishes? 'Certainly. I would, however, endeavour to influence them in other directions and would be sorry to think that I had promoted the purposes of the devil, with whom I have no sort of understanding at all.' But you must at least believe – indeed, you have often said so – that the 'masses' are 'better off' in some way with a knowledge of the arts than without it? 'Certainly I do, even if it is not a totally rational belief. The notion that you could get the majority of a population of 50 million to enjoy Wagner's operas, Shakespeare's plays or exhibitions of Impressionist painters is unreal, and even downright silly. Emerging from a performance of the *Ring* which you had invited them by some means to attend, the sole desire of very many would be to throw you into a horse-pond.'

Despite the risk of the horse-pond, however, you have spent much of your life canvassing the cause of greater access to the arts? 'Yes.' For no other reason than that they are good for you? Was there no more to it than that?

'The arts', G. replied, 'may open every kind of route to the best and most profitable forms of thought. My own life would have been an empty one but for the music, the plays and the paintings I have enjoyed. But it is a little sanguine to think that everyone who goes to a play or a concert is likely to be redeemed in some way.' To go to a concert or a gallery is like walking on the seashore in a bracing wind? 'That is a very good analogy. It is a good thing to do, good for people.' But what is it that is 'good' about a concert or an exhibition? 'When people are engaged in them they are prevented from being engaged in unworthy activities.' Is it your assumption that they otherwise would be? 'The theory of original sin has a certain amount of justification,' G. replied briefly.

So the virtue of the arts, despite what you have gained from them yourself, is essentially negative: those who are interested in them are for the time being not interested in something worse? 'That is not a negative virtue. If you had a lot of people engaged in picking oakum, they would be prevented from doing something worse, like stabbing their neighbours. But I would not regard picking oakum as a very virtuous activity because it has no future.' The arts are an alternative to picking oakum? 'There are many alternatives – skiing in Switzerland, for example – of which artistic activity is one.' All no more than a way of killing time? 'Every activity is a way of killing time. Climbing Everest is another.'

What you say may sound cynical, or perhaps despairing, yet you have been a notable patron of the arts, some might say a Maecenas. 'Only as far as my limited means permitted.' That, said I, conceals many great generosities of which the artistic world is aware. G. was silent for a moment, impassive. Is it not true? 'I have endeavoured to provide some support for particular artists.' Gladly? 'I do not think I am rich enough to bestow any money with joy. But if there is a moral need for it, there is a certain satisfaction in providing it.'

There are some who think, or claim, that creativity should be its own reward, said I. 'If one regards a particular artist as a worthy citizen, it is obviously necessary that he should be fed or he will be lost to starvation. It is also possible that a valuable artistic effort may fail for want of support.' Does the world then owe the artist a living, whether provided by the state or a generous individual? 'It obviously does not owe the artist a living. The artist cannot claim the world to be his debtor. But a worthy artist – not a singer who cannot sing, or a painter who cannot paint – obviously deserves to be supported; insofar as he or she lacks support, it reflects a shortcoming on society's part.'

Do you see yourself as part of a Jewish tradition of concern with, and patronage of, the arts? 'Over the generations, the Jews have discovered that one safeguard for them – not a total safeguard – is education. They have also discovered, with considerable perception, that education includes knowledge of the arts. Therefore, they will always be in the forefront of artistic interests and ventures.' You told me earlier that 'the rich, particularly Jews, are seldom interested in culture'. 'Rich Jews are only a small category of Jews. The Jews who have contributed most to culture are nearly always from the professional middle classes, and they are by no means always rich.'

But if they treat education and culture as a safeguard, however uncertain, that suggests they are not primarily interested in them for their own sake? 'Their concern is not a totally disinterested one. They have a predisposition to acquire knowledge which is portable. This is thoroughly reasonable for people who have been driven from home to home, and who cannot know from day to day when their next expulsion will take place.'

Much of your knowledge of the world of the arts is surely not portable at all? For example, is some of it not the fruit of your many personal friendships with artists? 'I acquired a lot of my knowledge through my friendships, especially with articulate artists such as Graham Sutherland and Lucian Freud, each of whom painted my portrait.' Who would you count as having been your closest artist-friends? 'Henry Moore was a good friend; Peggy Ashcroft was a good friend; John Barbirolli was a good friend. Yehudi Menuhin and Lucian Freud are good friends.' Have you found that artists make better friends than do others? 'The capacity for friendship is not determined by occupation, although it may make a person more attractive to you as a friend. It is determined by an individual's nature.'

But have artists made better friends than businessmen, say, or lawyers? 'They provided the possibility of interesting conversation, a possibility which does not exist – except very rarely – in contact with businessmen and lawyers.' Why not? 'Because I myself was interested in what the former were doing, and not very interested in what businessmen were doing.' But surely you were interested in what your fellow-lawyers were doing? 'Not really, not passionately interested,' G. replied.

13

Between Faith and Hope

Do you ever sigh and say, 'Ah, those were the days'? Do you feel nostalgia for times gone by? 'No. I feel no nostalgia for the past. But I have no dislike of the past either; it is not something to which I can take exception. In the past, time flowed by me just as does the present.' You have no sense of a lost 'Golden Age'? 'No, but I believe what every reasonable person believes: that there were aspects of the past of special glory, just as there are aspects of the present which are so.'

If everything flows by you, as you say, is all in flux? 'The basic emotions do not disappear, even if they are normally the less creditable ones which are the most constant.' But apart from the constant emotions, are there any 'eternal verities' – truth, virtue, beauty – which remain fixed for you in the tide of things? 'I certainly believe in a moral code which distinguishes between right and wrong, a distinction which is necessary to civilisation. One of society's troubles is that a generation is growing up for whom the distinction is not sufficiently defined,' G. added. Is the appreciation of beauty, say, not a universal, as well as an essential, thing? 'The appreciation of beauty is not as universal as it ought to be. But it has never been universal. Moreover, it was better established with the ancient Greeks than in subsequent ages,' G. replied shortly, as if not keen to continue in this vein.

Wouldn't you regard Truth as a noble ideal? 'I have nothing to say about it. It is obviously a quality to which people should aspire, and is fundamental to a well-ordered society.' There are some, said I, who would claim to have dedicated their lives to the search for it. 'That is a rather ridiculous statement,' G. rejoined with some impatience. 'It means that when you wake up and even before you have breakfasted, you must consider how to pursue the truth in the coming day.' You plainly don't like high-falutin' declarations of moral purpose. 'Emphatic declarations in favour of any philosophical system are to be avoided.' On principle? 'Because they give rise to great confusion: no two people are thinking of the same thing. And in a hard and ruthless world there is very little time to brood over philosophical matters.' Are you actually suggesting that it is *wrong* to do so? 'Such activity should be left to professional philosophers,' G. replied.

You can't be saying that you have never thought about such philosophical matters yourself? 'I cannot say that a large percentage of my time has been given over to large philosophical abstractions.' Some might define an intellectual as an individual with a taste for speculation about abstract ideals, the nature of truth included, said I. 'All honest people desire an unqualified *practice* of the truth,' said G. Does untruth cause you pain? 'Any situation where bad behaviour is involved causes one distress. Telling lies is not good behaviour, even if the entire political world, for instance, has become inured to it.'

You may shy away from discussing certain kinds of moral abstraction, I said, but in the course of our conversations you have attributed rather a lot to what you call

219

'the Almighty', and also seem prepared to leave a lot to Him. 'That was generous on my part,' said G. jocularly. 'I hope He will recognise it in due course. He has a heavy responsibility to do so.' A responsibility to you personally? 'To all of us,' G. replied. Why? 'Because everything which is manifestly wrong with our lives could be attributed to His responsibility, or rather to His irresponsibility.' I take it that that is less tongue-in-cheek than it sounds. 'It is not tongue-in-cheek at all. If this planet is governed by a universal force, it is not governed as it ought to be.'

Does this 'universal force' have a capital G? 'Certainly; I always respect a widespread general belief. Moreover, most people would stop short of denying the existence of God out of fear that they might be wrong. If He should turn out to have the powers some people attribute to Him, He could visit dire retribution upon them for having denied His existence.' Might it not be equally risky to attribute responsibility to God, as you momentarily appeared to do, for the world's woes? 'It might. There is an old Yiddish saying that "Man dare not say that God is wrong".' It is a wise axiom. But to blame Him one would also have to be a firm believer in His existence. If one believes in Him, it would also be sensible to believe that what He does is right by His own standards,' said G. wryly.

I cannot tell from your remarks whether you yourself believe in God or not. 'I have never seen any concrete evidence of His intervention in any affair. This is not a blasphemy but a simple fact. The supposition that He is a merciful Being is also not borne out by the facts.' You don't believe, then, that He parted the waves of the Red Sea for the fleeing Israelites? 'No, I do not,' G. cheerfully replied. 'The Red Sea clearly took upon itself the duty of letting the Israelites pass. But it was perhaps God who permitted the Egyptians to drown,' said G. with a laugh.

You take refuge in such ironies, said I. 'While I pay lip-service to a God, I am not entirely convinced of His existence. Indeed, it would be difficult for any rational being to be convinced by the bogus miracles upon which most religions insist. But looking around at the varieties of human kind, the animals, the plants, the fishes in the sea – the variety of this remarkable world – I do not believe that all this happened by pure accident.' It is a *non sequitur* to argue from that to a design and a Designer, I said. 'It is. But if you survey the scene there appears to be a pattern organised by a reasonable entity.' Do you address imprecations, or even maledictions, to this 'entity'? I interjected. 'No,' said G. flatly. 'I believe that there is something somewhere, which, even if it did not make a conscious decision in the matter, is responsible for the evolution of life as it has come about. Whether this has been a "supernatural" course of events must be the subject of argument for all time. But if it occurred as the result of a Darwinian process I should not regard that as an accident either.'

You do not wish to believe it was an accident? 'I should be embarrassed to believe it.' Do you *need* to believe that life has a 'definite purpose'? 'I would be doing myself less than justice if I believed that there was no controlling body or governing purpose behind this existence.'

Do you mean that you do not want to believe differently, since without such governing purpose our lives would be rendered absurd? 'The belief that there is a governing purpose would be rendered absurd. It would disappoint a lot of us,' G. added. 'But it would also be a strange human being who considered that everything which happens on this planet was planned.'

Perhaps your will to believe that all was not an 'accident' is an illustration of Gibbon's dictum that 'there is more pleasure in building castles in the air than on the ground'? 'That is to trivialise a rather important aspect of life,' G. replied with some asperity. 'Some sense of respect for the forces which produced mankind is a very desirable element in personal thought, and will operate to influence one's decisions to the good rather than the bad.' Are you saying that because you are, in some sense, 'God-fearing' you are a more moral person than you would otherwise be? 'That would require a belief in hell-fire, a belief which I do not have,' G. replied with a laugh. 'I do not believe that I will be consigned either to a blissful heaven or to an over-hot hell at the end of my brief span. I do not believe in an after-life, even though it might be a logical belief.'

Logical? 'On the basis that life is so short, and that only a mean force would have brought it into being without there being a further term.' That sounds less like logic than wishful thinking, said I. 'That is true, but there is a strong inclination to believe it because we arrive for a short span and depart under quite arbitrary conditions. What is there to believe about a divine purpose in this?'

Then logic suggests a 'second term', but not faith? 'This is getting into difficult territory. All this is a mystical form of speculation which is alien to my nature. I am very agnostic about an after-life. But no one would want to dissent from the promise of it lest they be wrong,' G. declared, levity returning. 'They would be immediately chided by the Almighty, or the Devil, for their want of confidence in them.'

Is this mixture of your beliefs, and lack of beliefs, strong enough to be called a faith? 'What is important to me is not what I believe but what I do not believe. I have a negative faith. I do not believe in the miracles associated with any religion. I do not believe that when Moses struck the rock water gushed forth nor that Jesus was the Son of God.' Where does your Judaism come into all this? 'My Judaism is a matter of loyalty rather than of faith,' G. replied.

'The most important consideration for a Jew is that one believes, or seeks to believe, in a single deity. The second, and arguably rather odious, belief is that the Jews are the "chosen people". Since I have had difficulty in identifying God, I have equal difficulty in identifying Who chose them. But when I look around it is clear to me that He had a limited choice.' You mean that God, in choosing the Jews, did the best of a bad job? 'If He weighed the thing up at all, it is not unreasonable to suppose that He had no real choice. The Jews are as good as any, and rather better than most.'

There is wryness – irony, or something deeply sardonic – lurking close below the surface of your replies, I remarked. There was a silence. 'Irony, or being sardonic, is a defence mechanism,' said G. He observed me for several moments in silence. 'One doesn't believe entirely in what one is saying. So one sends out smoke-signals not to be taken too seriously.' There is irony in that too, said I; it is generally possible to judge when you mean what you say, and when you do not. 'Most of the things I have said to you in the course of our conversations have been my honest beliefs. Among them is the belief that one should not take oneself too seriously. But in the situation in which you have placed me I am having to expect other people to take me seriously, and to spend real money – folding money – in order to secure some insight into what I believe.'

You are still being ironic. 'On the contrary. It is presumptuousness and conceit beyond justification.' Had you been a Desert Father, a Saint Jerome, you would have kept a Trappist silence at my approach? 'It would have been a more sensible policy than to think I had the answers to your questions.' Nevertheless, you have been answering them, and answering them well. 'I frame words,' G. declared. 'But using my own intelligence, I would regard many of my answers to you as unsatisfactory.'

Others, said I, will be the ultimate judges of that; I expect that today's conversation is making you uneasy, for being too 'mystical' or over-speculative? Do you prefer in general not to discuss the matters I have been raising with you?

'Yes, I do,' G. replied. Are you happier with your feet on the ground? 'I like to believe that I am a rational human being, influenced by considerations that are *there*. It may be that one cannot touch such considerations either, but as long as they are there, they provide a ground for orderly thought. I like to believe that my thoughts are orderly, measured and respectful of those things which are deserving of respect in this multifarious world. This may be a vain belief,' G. added characteristically, 'but I like to hold it.'

It suggests that for you certain forms of speculation are not deserving of respect. 'I feel impatient when nonsense is elevated to the status of serious thought.' What kind of nonsense? 'If I hear a powerful argument in support of the wisdom of an Indian *fakir*, or an assertion that my house is frequented by ghosts, this will undoubtedly irritate me.' Yes, but we were not speaking of ghosts and gurus, but of abstract or ideal speculation. 'I feel no impatience with philosophical discussion, however abstract, but I have no talent for it,' G. protested.

Nevertheless, there are clearly ideals which you espouse, and to which you aspire, even if you have a preference, or say that you have a preference, for the 'concrete', or what is 'there'. 'That is true. I would not attempt any definition of love, and less of pure love.* But it is a highly desirable ideal. It makes some human relations possible which would otherwise not be possible, even if most people – I emphasise most people, not everybody – are incapable of pure love, and although it gives rise to every kind of problem, mistake and injustice. "I love him" and "I love her" are assertions designed to rule out any sort of rational behaviour.'

Do you believe all emotions to be two-sided in this fashion, and therefore unstable as objects of human hope? 'The only stable emotions are the unpleasant emotions,' G. bleakly replied; 'jealousy, hatred, greed, these can be relied on to stay. But love, heroism, self-sacrifice, all these are ephemeral; in the case of love, belief to the contrary is a most common form of self-deception. A woman will continue to ask "Do you still love me, George?" when it is apparent to everyone outside St Dunstan's that he does not still love her.'

What you say argues a most pessimistic view of human nature. 'It does not. A pessimistic view would be one which governed your behaviour. Mine is governed by undue optimism,' said G., cheerfully enough. Is optimism always undue? 'It is undue if it is unrealistic, as when a man backs a horse or votes for a political party. Optimism about the outcome of such actions is seldom warranted.' But you are not so pessimistic as to think that everything man sets his hand to ultimately turns to dross and failure. 'No, but it does not follow that by your touching something it will turn to gold.' There is gold, however, is there not? 'There is gold, but it is undue optimism to believe

* I then asked G. what 'pure love' was; his answer is given in the Introduction.

that there is gold everywhere. The Klondike view of life is extremely suspect.' Despite your optimism? 'Yes.'

Frankly, because you disowned nostalgia so entirely, I cannot tell whether you think the world a better or worse place to be alive in than it was, broadly speaking. 'Are you speaking of England, China or Hawaii?' G. asked rhetorically, but with some irritation. 'Whatever I may think, it cannot be a universal thought, but only an individual thought. Moreover, my thoughts on such a question may be determined by the state of my digestion or an ingrowing toe-nail. The latter will not give rise to lofty judgments, but they will be real judgments for all that.' Nevertheless, said I, in the course of our conversations you have shaken your head often enough over various aspects of today's mores to suggest that you might think – sometimes, at least – that matters were going from bad to worse. 'There are often times when one shakes one's head,' responded G., with continuing irritation. 'But that does not indicate that I am making a comparison with times gone by.'

I fail to see, said I, why you should not. 'Because it is not a sensible thing to do,' G. answered with some curtness. Are you really saying to me that it is a waste of time to compare the present with the past? 'It is not a waste of time. People do it because it is enjoyable to do it. But by doing it one arrives at unscientific conclusions.' This seemed to me an extravagant assertion, sweeping away precedent and causation in its path, and I began to interject; the interjection was itself brushed aside. 'If you believe,' G. persisted, 'that things were worse in the past – obviously a false argument – this could lead you to the equally false assertion that the present situation approaches perfection. Conversely, the argument, also false, that things were so much better in the past might suggest that a quest for present improvement is unrealistic.'

In which case, one is disarmed from taking up every moral or social position which rests upon a judgment about the difference between past and present; judgments which you have made yourself. Could one not say, for example, that society is 'becoming more violent'? 'But what are you comparing it with?' G. expostulated. 'Ancient Greece? Ancient Rome? If you were a Huguenot, you would think it had been more violent on St Bartholomew's Day than any other day in your recollection,' G. declared, good humour returning. 'You must make selective judgments and choices in such matters.'

What I get from this, said I, is that you stubbornly refuse to be carried away by conventional argument. 'I would resist being carried away by any argument that was acceptable to a mob. Mob arguments have been arraigned by generations of thinkers.' True, and so they must. But you yourself made bitter reflection on the advance of 'greed' in these times, and that the times were the worse for it. Were you not also implying that in comparison with the past, there had been some kind of moral deterioration?

'In that particular respect, there has been.' And have things not gone from bad to worse in the media? 'The condition of the media is an example of a modern development which has placed them increasingly in the hands of not very socially conscious people, set on gain.' Nevertheless, you would not want to believe that the world is fuller than ever of unhappy, greedy, competitive and dissatisfied people, or that the 1950s, say, were more innocent or less lurid times.

'I do not believe,' G. replied, 'that there is a radical difference in the human creature in different generations. I think he is largely similar from generation to generation.

His behaviour, however, might vary insofar as it is regulated by convention. In King Arthur's day, you would get on your horse armed with a lance, and face an opponent armed with a similar, hopefully shorter, lance,' said G. with a laugh. 'Today, you would be likely to choose a different form of combat.'

Human nature, then, is the bogey, since it is incorrigible and unchanging? Is that what you would say? 'It would be wise to say it. Human nature cannot be changed. Human behaviour, however, can be changed but never for long, or securely; it slips back again to what it was.' Is the corollary of this that there is nothing to be newly surprised about in human conduct? 'It would have to be something really spectacular. For example, if I learned that the Eskimos had constructed a railway system entirely made from ice, I would be startled by the knowledge,' said G. light-heartedly. That is a trivial point, said I. You do not think that men, in their treatment of the natural world for instance, are guilty of new degrees of *hubris*? 'I would not respond to any suggestion that men should be judged *en masse*. The least that they can claim is to be judged as individuals,' G. replied with force.

There is nothing new under the sun, then, for a Jew to be anxious about? You are not kept awake by thoughts of acid rain? 'Acid rain does not keep me awake. Nothing keeps me awake which is the subject of a well-organised and illiterate lobby.' You will have the Greens chasing you up hill and down dale – or what is left of the dales – for that, said I. 'I am prepared to be chased by them.' But why are you so harshly dismissive of their case? 'I distrust fanatical statements about the "destruction of the planet", largely because I lack confidence in those bearing the message to me.' In other words, you reject the message *prima facie* because you do not like the look of the

messenger? 'I will not be persuaded to support any proposition on the basis of total ignorance about its truth. But
if the messenger is someone I admire, and in whom I have
faith, I will listen to his message.'

Are you inclined, in fact, to turn a blind eye to others'
breast-beating? 'I turn a blind eye to any argument which
is unintelligently or unconvincingly expressed.' What if it
is true? 'It is made more difficult for me to accept from the
nature of the argument and of the persons espousing it.'
You are prepared to measure the truth by the cut of a
man's jib? 'I might. It is not unreasonable to judge an
argument by the strength and reliability of its advocate.'
But on that basis you could espouse a cause simply because
you took a shine to the person who placed it before you?
'If an individual's doctrines were utterly abhorrent, I
would not be in the least impressed that the individual in
question looked like Adonis. The abhorrent nature of his
beliefs would destroy any interest in them, intellectual or
aesthetic. But although I have done my best to appear
inhuman,' said G. with heavy irony, 'some human attributes remain to me. One of them is to like certain people,
and on that account to be disposed to be persuaded by
them.'

Is that not irrational by your standards? 'It is not
irrational to be more persuaded by one's friends than by
one's enemies about how one should behave. I have very
few enemies. But I would reject an enemy's views of right
conduct, because he was an enemy,' said G. That still
does not sound a wholly rational judgment, said I; when
reason is in retreat – as now, once more, in attitudes to
the Jews – is it not a Jew's duty to be rational above all?

The question seemed, momentarily, to take G. aback. 'I
do not have a hopeful opinion that things are going to
change for the best,' G. suddenly said. In regard to the

Jews, or in general? 'In general, and especially in relation to lax attitudes to education. Today, in this country, you can find people without a single "O" level applying to be Archbishop of Canterbury, Prime Minister or Governor of the Bank of England. This is a serious backwards step.' Has there been a similar fall in standards of probity in public life, in your judgment? 'I have observed the development of a better power of concealing it,' G. replied. 'I do not think that there are fewer villains, or many more villains, but it is more difficult to expose a villain than it was, *vide* Robert Maxwell.'

I imagine, however, from what you said earlier, that you would not concede that people are behaving in a radically worse fashion, morally, than they were? 'Even a close study of the facts would not permit you to conclude that people are behaving better or worse than they were. However, if you ask a clergyman the same question he will opt for the answer that people are behaving worse.' Why should a clergyman think it, and not you? 'Because his criterion will be church attendance, and the churches are pretty well deserted,' G. replied with a laugh. 'Some might describe that as an escape from superstition, others as a serious moral deterioration,' he sardonically added.

Can anyone make progress in life without moral compromise? Could you? 'I do not know that I have attained such an inviolate moral position as to make the judgment. Moreover, I have rarely been presented with a powerful enough temptation. The principal temptation has been gastronomic.' To which you succumbed? 'To which I succumbed to some extent. But I was never offered a bribe in an attempt to get me to do something improper.' Nevertheless, do you think it is easy or hard to be both successful and good? 'It is hard to be good, full stop,' said

G., 'whatever that word may mean.' What do you think it means? 'It really means not noticeably bad,' G. answered.

But how can a man earn a reputation for sagacity, as you have done, without being shrewd or, to put it more plainly, cunning? 'If it's there, it's there,' was G.'s brief reply. But can a man be both successful and wholly benign, as many think you are? 'To be successful, in many walks of life, must involve compromise of a moral character,' G. conceded. 'I hope that in my own case – and others – such compromise was not the result of conscious decision, of a decision to be bad.'

Have you been bad? 'I would hesitate to *deny* that I had been bad. I can recollect events in the course of my life which were not particularly virtuous and which do not redound to my credit. I am not conscious of having cheated anyone, but I am not totally confident that I have not traduced people.' Wittingly or unwittingly? 'I hope never unwittingly; perhaps sometimes wittingly. The temptation to say nasty things about people is often irresistible, even in a character as splendid as mine.'

What you are speaking of sounds more like dinner-table gossip than sin. 'I would not set out deliberately to ruin anyone. But, on occasion, I would find it necessary to express powerful disapproval of what someone was doing, and might go too far in expressing my disapproval.' And that, said I, sounds like someone who considers himself morally superior, pronouncing *ex cathedra* on the frailties of others. Indeed, there have been times during our conversations, when you have come close to making such a claim. 'It would be totally hypocritical if I did not concede that I have made claims of superiority over some of my fellow-men.' Do you think you are justified in doing so? 'So many people are inadequate in intellectual and mental terms.' But do you consider yourself almost a saint? 'I have never arrived at that assessment of my moral conduct.' Nevertheless, I have heard you describe yourself as 'pure in heart'. 'I like to think I am,' said G. 'I can claim to be, at least comparatively, pure in heart, and in my estimation that is not a very high claim.' Some would think it the highest moral claim of all, I said. G. shrugged. 'By contemporary standards, my moral approach is as good as most,' he said.

You don't have feet of clay, like other men? 'I think that the reason why I claim a higher degree of morality than some others is that I am less susceptible to temptation. My personal life has always been led on a very modest scale. I never sought to emulate President Kennedy in having a new woman every day, or even every decade.' Do you regard that as some kind of constitutional strength in you, or what? 'We have to accept that we cannot define the reasons for most of our attributes, good or bad, just as I cannot say why my nose is a certain shape, my ears rather large, or my powers of persuasion well developed.'

Did you seek to set a moral example to others? 'No. I never tried to set a moral example, even if I hoped that people might have been influenced by my way of life, or by a desire to emulate it. It may be that I cannot claim to have been especially virtuous, but I can claim that I was not especially wicked.' How might the claim be tested? 'By my dislike of any form of violence, and my preparedness to give a helping hand to people whom I chanced upon. Today, a great part of mankind, seeing someone in trouble on the other side of the road, would avoid crossing the road. I am sufficiently a busybody to have crossed the road in 90 per-cent of cases.' When have you not crossed the road? 'When I have been on my way to the dentist with an appalling toothache.'

Your moral position seems to be this, said I: you have

sought to act morally yourself, you hope for moral improvement in the way the rest of the world wags, you believe you know how such improvement could be brought about, but you have no great confidence that it will be. 'You are a very unfortunate human being,' said G., 'if you have been born without any element of hope: one hopes that things will get better. I am also sufficiently clear-sighted to see how things could get better, but it does not prompt the belief that they will get better in a measurable period of time.' Plato thought a philosopher-king was required in such a predicament, and someone with a remarkable resemblance to himself. 'I am not in competition with Plato,' said G.

But whether all this makes you essentially an optimist or a pessimist, whatever you may say yourself about it, is a harder puzzle. In the course of our conversations, your disposition has been generally sunny, your remarks often amusing and wry, and we have laughed a good deal. It is also plain that you would prefer to be 'unduly' optimistic than unduly pessimistic, but Lucian Freud's portraits of you seem to show you melancholy and troubled. 'An artist portrays what he sees. When he was drawing me, Lucian Freud perceived a solemn element in my nature. But that does not preclude my other elements. I am largely of cheerful disposition.' There is no sign of cheerfulness or laughter in his portraits, said I. 'He is a remarkable artist, but he does not make many concessions to humour,' said G.

Did you not laugh with him, too, during your sittings for him? 'Indeed I did, and we had many happy conversations.' Then he must have consciously chosen the more sombre aspect. 'That is in his nature. He would not sit down to paint a *jolly* person. The word would be obnoxious to him.' Do you see yourself as a 'jolly person'? 'To say so might convey a rather vulgar impression, but I certainly see myself as more jolly than miserable,' G. replied.

Nevertheless, I recall when we were speaking *en passant* of happiness that you introduced the qualification 'insofar as one can be happy'. 'It is a sensible qualification. You can wake in the morning to hear the birds singing in the sunshine; within an hour or two, they can have ceased chirping and been driven off by the pouring rain. It is sensible to believe that the things which make you happy are ephemeral, and you must be reconciled to their disappearance.'

You even referred, once, to an unhappy person *in extremis* who wanted to escape 'this awful world'. 'That,' said G., 'was an expression of momentary feeling. My own world is not awful. On the contrary, it is good, promising, responsive and – to use an overworked word – civilised. It is a comfortable world where, although wealth does not abound, poverty is pretty remote from most of its participants. There is some suffering as a result of illness, but not so much illness in my circle as to think it in some way doomed.'

The circle revolves around you, does it not? 'Yes, it does. I am the common factor,' G. self-deprecatingly added. 'It is a very catholic circle, ranging from dustmen to dukes.' I have never encountered a dustman here, said I. 'No, there are no dustmen, but there are one or two dukes,' G. cheerfully conceded. 'It is also to a large extent regulated by the presence of people who need advice and assistance, and who come to me for that purpose.* Rather flamboyantly, I enjoy it.' Have you not had to overcome your own reserve in order to live in this fashion?

* On another occasion, G. said to me, 'Nobody ever comes to see me without a problem, or very rarely.'

'Yes, I was and remain to this day quite shy.' Shy of what? 'I am shy in making approaches to new people.'

Why? 'I am always conscious of the threat of being rebuffed. It does not make me a paranoiac, but it influences my social behaviour.' Do you mean that you fear you might not be liked? 'I do not think I have sufficient self-confidence to believe that people's basic emotion, when they meet me, will be to like me. This might be a disastrous error on my part, but I can think of more than two or three people who have shown a positive antipathy to me.' They expressed some kind of odium for you, or what? 'They indicated by their approach to me, or non-approach to me, that they did not like me.'

Were these experiences wounding? 'I would not say wounding, but disappointing.' You had been hoping to establish a rapport with these individuals? 'They were people who, in my usual blithe disregard of the realities, I confidently expected to like me.' But you have been supported emotionally by the liking of very many others? 'True. But it is equally true that, from time to time, I encounter someone who, as if by instinct, displays a want of affection towards me.'

To what do you attribute such responses? 'I believe the reasons to be principally political.' Political? 'I am associated – as it happens quite wrongly – with holding views in firm support of the Labour Party, God forbid. It is enough to lead a large number of convinced Tories to perceive me as a bitter enemy. They see me as a threat to their possessions.' Do you mean that you are tarred by your association with Harold Wilson? 'I am tarred by a left-wing brush.' When, in fact, you are both left and right, or neither? 'Exactly.' Could it be that you are seen by some as a Jewish crypto-leftist of famous archetype? 'What has worried people is not that I am a Jew but that I am attributed with holding opinions totally antagonistic to their ideas of private property. All political dislikes really hinge on ownership,' G. added; 'nothing scares a right-wing group so much as the fear that another group is after its property.'

But if you are misperceived by others, or puzzle them in one fashion or another, it is not all that surprising, said I. For instance, you are the leading solicitor of the day, yet you told me that you would rather have been 'anything but' a solicitor. Is it true? 'Yes, I think that is true.' What would you rather have done?

'I would have chosen to open the innings in a Test match, but the satisfaction of that would have lasted only one ball. I would also like to have been a professional psychiatrist; I already regard myself as an amateur psychiatrist.' What satisfaction would that have given you? 'I would have been engaged in an activity in which one can ameliorate human pain and suffering,' G. replied.

Have you not done that to any extent? 'It is possible for a solicitor perhaps once in a professional lifetime. It does not flow from your everyday activity to race to Pentonville to tell a poor client that he is not, after all, to be hanged. But my principal objection to being a solicitor was other solicitors. They are a very unimaginative and common-place lot.' As well as not being a solicitor, would you secretly rather have been an Englishman too? 'No. I wanted to be recognised as an "English Jew", despite all the contradictions which go with it.'

You would choose to be a Jew in another life? 'Those who know me know that the one thing I would never forswear is my Jewishness,' G. replied. There was a brief silence; our months of talking together were drawing to a close. I feel prouder now to be what I am, said I, and to share this 'thing' of Jewishness with you, than when we began our conversations. He looked at me intently for a few moments, with some emotion. 'I am glad to hear that. It is a good thing to hear. It is also a very great compliment; I thank you for it.'

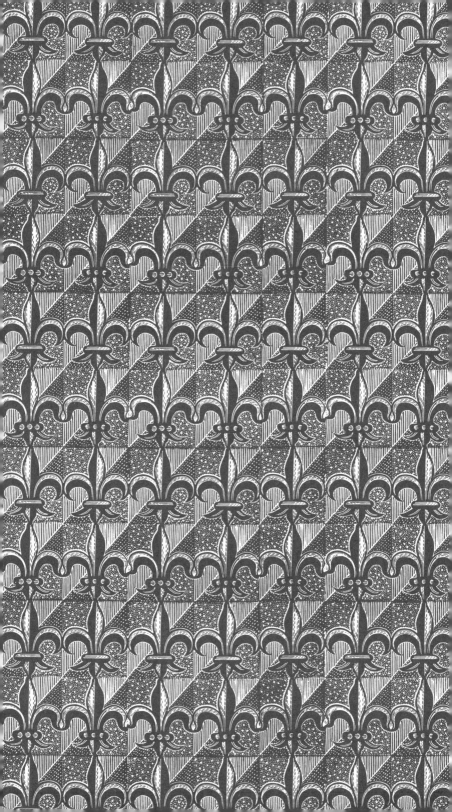